Possible Worlds

Possible Worlds

The Social Dynamic
of Virtual Reality Technology

Ralph Schroeder
University of London

■ WestviewPress
A Division of HarperCollinsPublishers

Cover Photos
Main photo: Ivan Sutherland's computer-driven head-mounted display (courtesy of
the University of Utah and Evans & Sutherland Computer Corporation).
Insets: Straylight's Virtual Reality Theater.

Published in 1996 in the United States of America by Westview Press, 5500 Central
Avenue, Boulder, Colorado 80301-2877, and in the United Kingdom by Westview
Press, 12 Hid's Copse Road, Cumnor Hill, Oxford OX2 9JJ

A CIP catalog record for this book is available from the Library of Congress
ISBN 0-8133-2955-8.—0-8133-2956-6(pbk.)

The paper used in this publication meets the requirements of the American National
Standard for Permanence of Paper for Printed Library Materials Z39.48-1984.

10   9   8   7   6   5   4   3   2   1

Contents

Figures

Acknowledgments

Several chapters in this book draw extensively on published essays. These are all listed in the bibliography and I am grateful to the various publishers for permitting me to make use of this material here.

Thanks must go, above all, to Bryan Cleal and Warren Giles, who spent many months as participant observers in a number of settings where VR is being developed and used. I am also grateful to those who allowed Bryan and Warren to work with them: Michael Clark of the West Denton High School, Peter Dzwig at the London Parallel Applications Centre, Andrew Nimmo and Mel Slater of the computer science department at Queen Mary and Westfield College, Ian Andrew and colleagues at Dimension International, John Wilson and Sue Cobb of the Nottingham University Virtual Reality Applications Research Team, David Steward of the Shepherd School, Simon Rushton and Robin Taylor of the Department of Psychology at Edinburgh University, and Mike Bevan of *VR News*.

It is also a pleasure to acknowledge the generosity of my hosts and discussion partners. Linda Houseman at the University of North Carolina at Chapel Hill and Ann Elias at the University of Washington's Human Interface Technology Laboratory kindly helped with my arrangements for visiting these institutions. Terry Rowley took the time to give me an informative tour of W Industries. Dutch Guckenberger supervised my F-16 flight and Steve Benford and his colleagues introduced me to networked Doom, among other things. I am grateful to Stephen Ellis of NASA Ames Research Center, Mike Moshell of Institute for Simulation and Training at the University of Central Florida, Pavel Curtis at the Xerox Palo Alto Research Center (PARC), and Warren Robinett for providing friendly interfaces to a nonspecialist. Shinji Tanaka made my visit to Japan most enjoyable, and Katzutomo Fukuda of Fujitsu, Susumu Tachi of the University of Tokyo, and Norihiko Matsuura of the Nippon Telegraph and Telephone Human Interface Laboratories (NTT) were likewise generous hosts.

My conversations with David Leevers at BICC invariably took me into new realms of thinking about VR. Robin Hollands of Sheffield University and Roy Kalawsky of Loughborough University saved me from several errors in Chapter 2, and Klaus Boehm of the Fraunhofer Institute carefully looked over Chapter 3. Martin Greenwood kindly improved the penultimate draft. I would also like to thank the eagle-eyed editors at Westview Press for their amazing work in making the text more readable. Former colleagues at Brunel University, and especially Eric Hirsch and Tom Osborne, will disagree with the tone of the book, but I hope they won't be disappointed by the degree to which they have helped me to avoid an all too narrow viewpoint. Thomas Heimer of the Johann Wolfgang Goethe University and Leslie Haddon of Sussex University were very generous with their expertise in the sociology of new technologies. I wish I could say that others have contributed to the errors and omissions in this book, but, in fact, the blame is mine alone.

Without Brunel University's Research Initiative Fund this project, literally, would not have gotten off the ground, and I would like to thank the university for this excellent method of supporting research. John Richardson was as supportive a head of department as I could have wished for during this period. On a personal note, I owe an enormous debt to Anne, who made my weekends more productive and enjoyable. Finally, Jennifer, Sven, and Anja can rest assured that I will now emerge from my HMD.

Ralph Schroeder

Possible Worlds

1

Virtual Worlds and Sociological Knowledge

Until the early 1990s, the term virtual reality was practically unknown. Then around 1991–1992, stories began to appear in the media about a revolutionary technology that allowed people to enter computer-generated worlds using a helmet and glove. Since that time, virtual reality systems have become commonplace, attracting hundreds of researchers and developing into a sizable industry. And although, until recently, these systems were so expensive that only large research laboratories could afford them, virtual reality has now become poised to enter the home in the form of virtual shopping and computer games. As with other new technologies, the emergence of virtual reality has raised many questions about its social implications, especially as there now seems to be a possibility that virtual reality may become a medium for communication.

This book has two aims: The first is to provide a sociological account of the emergence and the implications of virtual reality systems. Or, to put it in the form of a question, what are the social forces that have shaped virtual reality technology and how is the technology, in turn, shaping social life? In this sense, the book is a case study in the sociology of technology and, more specifically, of new information and communication technologies. The second aim is to relate this case study to more general theoretical issues in the sociological study of technology. As we shall see, there are still fundamental theoretical disagreements in this area. I shall thus use virtual reality to develop a model of the relation between technology and social forces that addresses some of these disagreements and may, I hope, point the way beyond them.

Virtual reality, or VR, is often taken to refer to a computer linked to a head-mounted display and a glove. VR systems give the user a sense of being inside a computer-generated environment and of being able to interact with it. The label "virtual reality," however, has also been attached to simulator rides in arcades or to 3-D images displayed on desktop computers. Phrases like the "virtual community," the "virtual corporation," or indeed "virtual sex" have proliferated. Academic researchers, meanwhile, have shied away from using the term "virtual reality" and often prefer "virtual environments" or "synthetic environments." They argue that the worlds created by VR technologies are far from "realistic" and so have created confusion and encouraged unfulfillable expectations. However we may come to define VR (and we shall do so after presenting a brief history of VR in the next chapter), it is a technology that is still in the process of taking on a firm shape.

The problem of labels has also arisen because it is difficult to maintain a clear separation between research carried out in VR and developments in other fields such as artificial intelligence, computer-aided design, interactive television, and computer-mediated communication. It may be that the expectations generated by the alleged "convergence" of computer-based information and communication technologies has blurred the boundaries among these technologies. As we shall see, from the point of view of assessing the social implications of VR, it will make sense to compare some of these new technologies side by side. Even if VR occupies only a small niche on the "electronic frontier," there is little doubt that it is among a number of technologies that are changing rapidly and playing an increasingly important part in our lives.

How, then, should we set about examining the significance of this technology? Social scientists have in recent years devoted much attention to new information and communication technologies. Yet there has been little consensus within the various disciplines involved about how to explain the role of communications media, human-computer interfaces, or scientific and technological advances in general. To give just one example, there seems to be little common ground between technological determinists like Marshall McLuhan (1964) and Daniel Bell (1979), who argue that new technologies have radically transformed society and that we now live in a "global village" or an "information society,"[1] and others, such as Bruno Latour (1993) and Donna Haraway (1991), who believe that because scientific and technological artifacts are always already influenced by our cultural understandings of them, they can have no autonomous logic or influence of their own. To examine VR, it will therefore be necessary to address these larger debates concerning the role of technology in society.

Before we begin with an overview of the content of the book, it may be useful to touch briefly on this theoretical side of the book. Despite the lack of consensus in the sociology of science and technology, in recent years there has been one dominant approach, or rather a cluster of approaches, which has come to be known as the "the sociology of scientific knowledge," or the "social shaping of technology."[2] This cluster shares a basic assumption with much current theoretical discussion in the social sciences, whether this comes under the labels social constructivism, deconstruction, or postmodernism: namely, a rejection of realism, or the notion "that there is a world to be investigated which exists independently of human belief and language" (Trigg 1993:6).

One of the purposes of this book is to challenge the antirealist view in the study of technology and of the social world. I will argue that unless we agree that knowledge is separate from the reality to which it refers, neither the genesis nor the consequences of new technologies can be explained. In fact, without realism, it is impossible to say that scientific or technological advance has taken place and, thus, that changes in the social world have resulted from this advance. The approach to the role of technology in society that follows from a realist baseline (one that I will try to develop here in relation to virtual reality technology), by contrast, departs in a fundamental way from existing approaches in the field. Inasmuch as the approach I take also differs from technological determinism, the main theory that preceded the "sociology of scientific knowledge" and "social shaping," it tries to advance the way technology is discussed in the social sciences.

There is a further twist to this story that we shall need to pursue and that also needs to be mentioned briefly. One by-product of virtual reality and related technologies is that they themselves have become part of the inspiration for current theoretical thinking in the social sciences. Because these technologies supposedly make our social world somehow less real, they currently inform much thinking about the blurring of boundaries between nature and culture, between humans and nonhumans, and the like. These latest incarnations of postmodern antirealist ideas have come to be known as "cyberculture" and its favorite adjective is "virtual" (Escobar 1994). The approach in this study, again, differs on a very basic level from these antirealist modes of thought. But as we are concerned with virtual reality, we shall need to look at these postmodern ideas as part and parcel of the range of cultural phenomena that have sprung up around this technology.

These theoretical debates about the sociological study of technology will be discussed further in the first and the final chapters of the book. The main part of the book, however, is devoted to a sociological investigation of VR; that is, to the social conditions of the emergence of this technology and the various settings in which it is being developed and used. A brief overview of these chapters follows.

Chapter 2 will present a brief history of VR. In the 1960s, Ivan Sutherland proposed a computer display with which users could interact. This display, he said, would one day be so realistic that "a bullet displayed in such a [computer simulated] room would be fatal" (1965:508). Subsequent work on this technology was primarily pursued in the context of flight simulation and other scientific and military programs. Thus "virtual reality" did not become widely known until the early 1990s, when a number of research institutes and firms began to produce interactive computer displays. There has since been increasing competition to develop high-powered VR systems and to exploit the large potential market for VR applications. Tracing the history of the technology from the early research on computer displays, flight simulators, and human-computer interaction, this chapter will provide the background to the proliferation of VR systems in the 1990s.

The second half of Chapter 2 will give an overview of the technical aspects of VR systems. The early research effort has produced a variety of input/output devices for human interaction with computing systems. These devices, combined with the increase in relatively low-cost computing power in the 1980s, accounted for the accelerated development of sophisticated VR systems in the early 1990s, including systems that allow shared virtual worlds. Apart from giving a brief description of the main technical components of VR systems, we shall need to get a sense of the range of devices that are available and of the major changes in performance and cost. VR development has been uneven as well as constrained by such factors as the state of computer graphics capabilities, for example, and by human factors issues such as simulator sickness. The degree to which these obstacles have been overcome varies between systems and components and we shall see how advances and constraints in VR continue to shape the technology to this day.

In Chapter 3, we shall examine the research and development context of VR, from the laboratories to the making of devices for a consumer electronics market. VR has given rise to a research effort involving hundreds of researchers and dozens of laboratories and firms. This rapid mobilization of resources has been premised on the belief that VR will play an integral part in the expected transformation of information technologies and communications networks. Some of the key research institutes and firms developing VR will be examined in order to show how advances in technology are spurred by the links and the competition between them. This means comparing their strategies and the different forms of collaboration between research and industry that, in turn, need to be set in the context of the different national agendas for developing advanced technology. At the same time, the thrust of VR development is shifting away from research laboratories and toward the consumer electronics market, with multinational companies hoping to make VR into a mass-market product. To see how research and development efforts shape VR technology, we shall also look at a concrete instance of how this shaping takes place in several labs. Here we can use the example of how the body is represented in the virtual world, one of the key issues in VR research.

Chapter 4 will examine two applications of VR, in entertainment and education. As yet there are few settings in which VR is used on an everyday basis, but there have been a number of projects that have used VR for teaching. Three education projects will be examined here—a special needs school, a VR summer school, and a school following the standard British curriculum. These VR applications invite comparison with other educational uses of information technology, as well as providing an opportunity to analyze everyday modes of interaction with VR systems and pupils' responses to creating virtual worlds. Moreover, in this context it is possible to assess the benefits of interacting with virtual worlds compared with other modes of learning, particularly as the projects under consideration represent very different learning environments.

The most widespread usage of VR, however, has been in entertainment, particularly in arcade games that feature interactive adventures. And although the emergence of VR games can be traced to other computer and video games, the way in which players interact with virtual worlds also brings a new dimension to this form of entertainment, as it provides an experience that is in some ways more engrossing than other games. VR games have also provoked well-publicized concerns among the public about the health and safety of the games and about computer "addiction."

A different way of looking at VR is to bracket the question of the context in which the systems are used and to focus exclusively on the content of virtual worlds. Such an examination of virtual worlds, from within, will be the subject of Chapter 5. Approaching the virtual world from within is all the more important because, as the use of VR systems multiplies, users may come to spend extensive periods within virtual environments, either singly or in shared virtual worlds. Hence, it may be useful to explore the shape of these worlds at the outset: what mode of navigation is employed, how the interaction between multiple users is construed, and which aspects of the real world are incorporated into virtual worlds. Examining these and other features of VR will allow us to ask how the user experiences these worlds as "real."

Pursuing these questions about VR will also help us to establish what the most common features of virtual worlds are. Although virtual worlds currently provide only limited (primarily visual and auditory) experiences of "worldlike" environments, the differences between these worlds—for instance, the difference between flying and walking modes of navigation, between worlds with a high degree of "realism" compared with those in which the user feels immersed because of the nature of the interaction, between imaginative worlds and worlds that simulate real-life processes, or between single- and multi-user worlds—already yield a number of clues about what makes them interesting or enjoyable (or the opposite). Set against other modes of human-computer interaction and other uses of information and communication technologies, the exploration of virtual worlds from within points to an important shift in the way in which we interact with new technologies.

In Chapter 6 we will turn to the cultural phenomena associated with VR technology. VR has quickly gained a subcultural following, which includes devotees of science fiction literature, computer game enthusiasts, and computer "hackers." The futuristic ideas of cyberpunk or cyberculture, which manifest themselves in magazines and clubs, for example, also mirror, as I have mentioned earlier, contemporary theoretical movements within the academic world, such as "cyborg postmodernism." These academic trends are inspired by the possibilities offered by the artificial worlds created by information and communication networks and by the way in which these networks may allow for new forms of cultural expression.

At the same time, cyberculture promotes an alternative understanding of the role of technology that aims to subvert military and corporate uses and seeks instead to use the technology to explore novel forms of consciousness suited to a new age in which science merges with art and technology and becomes a tool for the political imagination. These visions of a world that is transformed by information and communication networks, in which cyberspace and VR play a prominent part, can be seen as part of a wider rethinking of the role of technology in society: if technology is no longer unambiguously associated with progress, machines that can enhance human creativity and interpersonal relations are nevertheless perceived as the key to cultural renewal.

Finally, in Chapter 7, we will return to the theoretical concerns that were raised at the outset. This can be done by considering how the various aspects of VR that have been examined add up to a larger whole. In the conclusion, I shall argue that existing approaches to new technologies overlook the fact that the relation between technology and social life operates on several interconnected levels that require a combination of sociological perspectives. At the macro level, the development of VR technology must be attributed to scientific and technological advances that are autonomous from social forces. At the same time, VR must be situated within a wider transformation among information and communication technologies. The social implications of VR can therefore only be established by reference to both scientific and technological factors and by comparison with other, similar technologies.

But it is also necessary to investigate the micro level; that is, to compare the experiences with VR and the responses to the technology in a variety of settings and to determine how these experiences and responses point to the way in which artifacts are becoming embedded in everyday life. The reception of VR on the micro level and the cultural phenomena and debates that the introduction of VR technologies has provoked, in turn, can be seen to signal a shift in attitudes toward the social role of technology and in the relation between humans and machines. It is only by bringing these macro and micro perspectives together that we can understand the social dynamic of this technology, which is a precondition for thinking about its implications and the options for future development. If, on the way toward explaining the background and the implications of the development of VR, a "realist" standpoint is able to shed some light on the relation between technology and society generally, it will also be possible to advance beyond the seemingly intractable theoretical disputes that have dominated this important area of social science.

The Sociology of New Technologies

Machines are frozen spirit. (Weber 1980:332)

Before grappling with VR itself, we shall need to outline the position taken here with regard to the sociology of new technologies, both because this is such a controversial area and because one aim of this book is to use VR to engage with these controversies. Studies of technology within the social sciences have been conducted under a variety of disciplinary headings. There are, for example, studies within economics of the impact of technological innovation (Freeman 1987), anthropological case studies of technologies in particular settings (Pfaffenberger 1992), the "social shaping" approach within sociology (MacKenzie and Wajcman 1985), and examinations of new technologies from the perspective of media studies (Rogers 1986). Moreover, within each discipline, there is a range of viewpoints. Presenting an account of these points of view would take up a book-length study in itself. I will suggest later that it is necessary to draw on a number of perspectives within the disciplines mentioned, but instead of making that case here, it will be more useful to focus on how the present study departs from existing approaches. To do this, we can briefly go into what is perhaps the most fundamental and divisive issue in the sociology of technology; namely, the relation between technology and social change.

   The issue of how technology is linked to social change is unavoidable in the study of technology, but there is little by way of consensus here. It is possible to say without too much simplification that explanations of science and technology within social science have typically taken two forms: on the one side, there are those who take the view that science and technology cause social change. With regard to technology, this view is sometimes labeled technological determinism and is associated with the notion that technologies follow trajectories. With regard to science, the idea is that scientific knowledge is subject to criteria that are universal or independent of reality, which implies that there is an irreversible advance in scientific knowledge. This school of thought rests on the premise that scientific and technological forces are autonomous and apart from society.

On the other side are those whose view could be described as social determinism, a term that can be used to subsume the labels of the "social shaping of technology" or the "sociology of scientific knowledge." The social determinist viewpoint has come to overlap, to a large extent, with postmodern ideas in the social sciences. Here, the central idea is that technology is necessarily a product of social or cultural forces and that technological change should never be seen as an independent agent, but always in its social context. Similarly, as regards science, the argument is that scientific knowledge can never be divorced from its social or cultural context and that it is therefore impossible to detach the validity of this knowledge from its social or cultural determinants.[3]

As with many intractable debates in the social sciences, it is tempting to say that there must be some truth on both sides, but the situation is more complex than that. I shall argue that resolving the dispute between the technological and social determinists is possible only by recognizing that there are different types of interplay between technological and social forces on different levels, which means that in order to understand the social implications of new technologies, we must combine these levels. One way to approach resolving the dispute is to distinguish different kinds of questions that can be asked in explaining the relation between science, technology, and society.

The first is the macro-sociological question concerning the role of science and technology in industrial or modern society as a whole. At this level, there is much to be said for scientific and technological determinism because, to begin with the case of science, scientific knowledge has grown exponentially since the scientific revolution. Moreover, the resulting stock of valid or objective scientific knowledge that has accumulated in this way is reproducible in all social contexts. Thus, the growth of scientific knowledge rests not on social factors—although it is true that certain social preconditions existed that were favorable to the first emergence of modern science—but on the validity of scientific method.

Similarly, there is no doubt that technological innovation has occasioned social change on the macro-sociological level. Among economic historians, there has been an ongoing debate over whether such changes should be understood, for example, from an evolutionist or saltationist (proceeding by leaps) perspective.[4] Nevertheless, it remains the case that technological innovation is one of the key causal factors in explaining economic growth throughout industrial societies. (It can be added that economic growth is singled out here only because more research has been done on this aspect as opposed to, say, the influence of technology on warfare or on communications.) Given that fact, we can say that technology has shaped industrial or modern society inasmuch as there has been a steady (which is not to say uniform) advance of technological innovation.

In both cases, the claim is not that it is impossible to explain particular instances in the advance of scientific knowledge or of specific technologies in terms of the social context in which they arose. It may well be that individual innovations are a response to particular social needs. The more important point, however, is that the overall success of science can ultimately be explained only by reference to a universally valid method. The growth of scientific knowledge, in turn, is a necessary—but perhaps not sufficient—precondition for technological advance, and both are responsible for a host of social changes that set industrial societies apart from preindustrial ones (although the relation between science and technology, which is more complex than has just been indicated, will be discussed more fully later in this chapter).

What has all this to do with explaining the social role of specific new technologies? Assuming that what has been said so far is correct, it will be possible to ask about the origins of technological innovation only in a broad sense, specifying the general conditions (resources, skills, and the like) that constitute the basis for scientific and technological advance. If these advances have consisted of a genuine growth of knowledge or an enhanced grasp of reality, however, it will be impossible to "reduce" them to social factors.

The same applies to technology, except that, in this case, it is necessary to point to an enhanced ability to manipulate the natural or social worlds. Hence technological advance, too, is in this sense irreducible to social factors or social shaping. The immediate corollary is that it will be necessary to examine not only the broad forces that shape scientific and technological advances but also their impact or consequences.

At this point, it may be useful to recapitulate and spell out the implications of what has been argued so far. Apart from asking about the general conditions that make science and technology possible, it is also necessary to examine their social implications. How this can be done will be spelled out in due course. But, in any case, these implications result from the fact that science and technology, on the macro level, are independent of social factors. If this seems an obvious point to make, it should be noted that the schools of thought that have been grouped here under the social determinist label—such as the sociology of scientific knowledge, the social or cultural shaping of technology, and postmodernism in its various forms—systematically exclude the possibility of (autonomous) technological advance and its impacts, since they conceive of science and technology as social or cultural constructions.[5] A different way of highlighting this shortcoming of the social or cultural shaping schools is that they necessarily begin and end with the local context of science and technology, in contrast to the universalism or irreversibility of scientific and technological advance that is being recommended here.

This is a good point at which to turn briefly to the issue of the relation between science and technology. As Collins has pointed out, the relation between the two has been historically variable (1986: 111–115). The widely held view that technology is "applied science" can, for example, be stood on its head inasmuch as technological advances in research instruments have often paved the way for scientific advance (Collins 1994:162–165).[6] Moreover, in the postwar period, science and technology have perhaps been more intertwined than ever, and thus some social scientists have used the label "techno-science." In VR, too, it is difficult to disentangle the contributions of, say, computer science from refinements to the computer hardware. What matters, in this case, as I shall argue shortly, is the separability of science and technology on the one hand and physical and social reality on the other. Thus I shall mainly speak of scientific and technological advance (instead of techno-science and innovation) since the relation between science and technology cannot be abstracted from the various levels of investigation.

At this stage, we can return to contemplating the different levels of technological change and ask, what of the micro level? With respect to this level, we are likely to be interested in different issues. Instead of asking about the validity of scientific knowledge or about the relation between innovation and economic growth, it will be more relevant to ask how particular technological artifacts become embedded in particular social contexts, how users experience these new tools, and how the users' social relationships change as a result. This applies particularly to new technologies, despite the fact that in the case of new technologies, unlike, say, with the automobile or television, it is not yet possible to discern the impact of the widespread adoption of these new tools. Precisely for this reason, however, it is all the more important to identify the early seeds of change, since later changes are often prefigured in the very early uses of a technology. This is especially important in investigating an area such as information and communication technologies or VR, in particular, which affect users directly, as opposed to "large technological systems" (Hughes 1987) like electricity or space flight, in which the consequences for users may be mediated in various ways.

This point can be made in a different way. Even when we are dealing with particular settings at the micro level, we shall need to see how these settings are shaped by and add up to more wide-ranging changes. Such an aggregation of settings, however, returns us to the macro level, since going from particular instances of the use of a technology to more widespread uses means giving an indication of a general direction or trend in which scientific and technological advance is moving: in other words, how particular technologies fit in with or compare with other technologies, in which social settings the technologies become more prevalent, and how they transform these settings or become transformed by them.

An interesting point that immediately arises from the discussion of the macro and micro levels is that it is at the meso level, the level of institutions or organizations, that we would expect to find the greatest degree of integration between the two perspectives, and it only requires a moment's reflection to confirm that this is so.[7] It is in the institutions that are engaged in research and development of new technologies that the autonomous logic of technological advances—the advances made in improving the capabilities of the devices—come together. And in these same institutions, the social constraints and opportunities—such as the decision to pursue one line of research rather than another or the decision about what resources can be devoted to particular projects; in short, the different trade-offs within and between the social on one side and the scientific and technological on the other—also coalesce.

So far, the approach that will be argued for here has been advanced in terms of a distinction between a number of levels and how they might be linked. At this point, we can return to the implications of technological advance by establishing more specifically what kinds of processes need to be examined at these levels. As indicated in the previous section, the sociological (and ultimately philosophical, as we shall see in a moment) position that I argue for is a "realist" one. I maintain that the extremes of technological determinism and of social determinism can only be avoided by taking into account both the growth of scientific knowledge and the material makeup of technological artifacts, on the one hand, and the social settings in which they become embedded, on the other.

If we adopt this perspective, we need to begin by asking: Where do the advances in virtual reality technology come from? As we shall see in the next chapter, advances in what VR systems allow users to do depend to a large extent on a number of improvements to VR hardware and software: accurate position-trackers, high resolution stereoscopic viewing devices, and increasingly realistic three-dimensional computer graphics. These improvements, in turn, have been made possible by scientific and technological advances in a number of fields that include magnetic sensors, liquid crystal and cathode-ray tube displays, and increased computer processing power. The general difficulty in the sociology of science and technology, however, has been to translate such advances and refinements into an account of the changing relations between artifacts and social life.

In producing such an account, I find it useful to draw on Hacking's philosophy of science. Hacking has argued that modern science "has been the adventure of the interlocking of representing and intervening" (1983:146). "We shall count as real," he writes, "what we can use to intervene in the world to affect something else, or what the world can use to affect us" (1983:146). This idea can be extended to the sociology of technology. Paraphrasing Hacking, we can say that technology has been the adventure of the interlocking of refining and manipulating, except that, in this case, manipulating the world "to affect something else, or what the world can use to affect us" takes place through artifacts or, in other words, takes place through techniques related to the physical world or to material objects. Here I follow Agassi, who has argued that "at the very least . . . the implementation of any technique whatsoever involves both physical and social activities" (1985:25). Or, to put it differently, technological artifacts are always in some sense ("physical") hardware.

The implication is that the dynamic of technology should be analyzed at the level of concrete processes of refining and manipulating, demonstrating how different artifacts achieve different effects on the natural and social worlds. To do this, it is necessary to identify the range of technological options available in the case of a particular artifact—and thus the range of its effects. It then becomes possible to make comparisons both between the effects of the chosen artifact in different social settings and between the effects of this artifact and those of similar artifacts that are being used in related social settings (or to make a comparison with social settings in which no technological means are employed). It will also be possible to assess how the range of this artifact is becoming narrowed or widened, which is a particularly crucial issue in the case of new technologies.

In short, it will be possible to evaluate in what sense a particular technology has a distinctive or cumulative impact, an impact that can be traced through the various social contexts in which the technology becomes embedded. It is therefore not just scientific and technological advances that have to be taken into account but also the social side of these advances. Here, in parallel to Hacking's "representing and intervening," Weber's notions of "rationalization" and "disenchantment" are useful, since they capture the two sides of social processes that inevitably accompany scientific and technological advancement: the spread of instrumental-rationality (or of using the most efficient means to achieve a given end) and the increasing impersonality of the external conditions of life.[8] When we examine the role of specific technologies, however, it will be necessary to bring Weber's ideas about large-scale social processes down to the level of everyday life; that is, to look at the concrete social settings in which the technology is used and how rationalization and disenchantment take place on this level.

This last point brings us back to the discussion of levels and their relation to "realism." I shall suggest that it is impossible in the sociology of science and technology to establish at the outset which level should be given priority and, thus, which level to single out in order to assess the implications of new technologies. This impossibility stems from the fact that it is unclear what types of artifacts or sets of social relations will be crucial to the process of social and technological development. In this respect, the sociology of technology is different from other areas within sociology that focus on certain entities, like states and classes on the macro level or face-to-face interaction on the level of smaller-scale changes, that are given as the objects of enquiry. All that can be said in the case of scientific and technological advance is that certain types of processes can be observed on different levels and are responsible for the social implications of new technologies.

In the case of the sociology of new technologies, these processes, again, are those of refining and manipulating, on one side, and rationalization and disenchantment on the other. The relationship between technology and society is thus a dynamic one. As a result, it is only when the various levels are finally interrelated, at the end of our study, that we shall come to understand the "reality" of scientific and technological advances and the "reality" of the social settings in which they have become embedded. Perhaps the main obstacle to overcoming the divide between technological determinism and social determinism has so far been that they have adopted a one-sided approach to the question of which level of social and technological development to regard as "real."

Finally, some comment is necessary about the method of research of this study. As the aim here is to interrelate various levels of VR development, the approach that I have adopted is to gather as much information as possible about all the key aspects of VR. In deciding which areas to focus on, I have drawn on studies of new technologies from a range of social science disciplines. I have also kept abreast of the scientific and technical literature in this field; interviewed researchers, developers, and VR users; and visited laboratories, firms, and various settings where VR is being used. In addition, I employed two research assistants, who each spent a total of ten months in six settings where VR is researched, developed, and used—a computer science department, a software firm, a psychology department, a high school, a special needs school, and a VR newsletter. Whether this mixture of using published sources, interviews, and participant observation has been adequate to the tasks I have set out here may be judged at the end of this study.

2

From the Ultimate Display
to Reality Built for Two
and Beyond

Origins and Lull

The term "virtual reality" was coined by Jaron Lanier in the late 1980s (Rheingold 1991:15–16), but the origin of virtual reality technologies can be traced back to Ivan Sutherland's work on interactive computing and head-mounted displays in the mid-1960s (Ellis 1991:325; Palfreman and Swade 1991:95–97). As we shall see in a moment, there were a number of forerunners to Sutherland's work in entertainment and other technologies. It is Sutherland's work, however, that has provided the foundation for much of the subsequent research related to VR. Sutherland was based at the Massachusetts Institute of Technology (MIT) and Harvard and partly funded by the Defense Department's Advanced Research Projects Agency (DARPA).[1]

In a paper he contributed to the International Federation of Information Processing Congress in 1965, entitled "The Ultimate Display," he outlined a model for human-computer interfaces that has continued to inspire the thinking about computer-generated virtual environments ever since (Sutherland 1965:506–508). His idea was for a computer display that would simulate the physical world and that the operator could interact with directly by means of the senses. Such a display would offer new possibilities for displaying complex information. In a subsequent paper presented at the Fall Joint Computer Conference in 1968, he explained how "a head-mounted three-dimensional display" could be built using a position sensor plus computer graphics to generate a three-dimensional world (Sutherland 1968:757–764). Sutherland moved to the University of Utah and by

January 1, 1970, together with a team of researchers, had developed the first operational interactive head-mounted display system (Rheingold 1991:106). (See Figure 2.1.)

Several things are noteworthy about Sutherland's "ultimate display." One is that his research was conducted under the auspices of the American military establishment (Palfreman and Swade 1991:192). Military funding contributed to the emergence of microelectronics research and development in the United States generally (Molina 1989). But unlike some other areas of computing that were directly relevant to military applications, Sutherland's system, which was the first to use computer graphics for interaction between the user and the machine, was thought of as an all-purpose means for interacting with computers for applications like information display and training for spacecraft docking operations. These applications contrast with, say, research on high-speed computing, which was driven, to a certain extent, by nuclear weapons development (MacKenzie 1991).

Another feature of Sutherland's head-mounted display was that it utilized half-silvered mirrors as screens so that the user could see the display and the real world at the same time.[2] Almost all the systems currently in use, by contrast, do not allow users to look at the real world. Furthermore, because of the limitations on computing power, the objects in the three-dimensional display were represented by means of wire frame graphics—that is, they were represented in outline. Another feature in Sutherland's system was that the head-mounted display was attached to a mechanical arm that relayed the position of the user's head to the computer. This was a simple device compared with current position-trackers, but one that worked within the limitations of the technology available at the time. Regarding interaction with the display, what is remarkable about Sutherland's early system is the degree of interaction that it permitted. In a virtual environment that was created for simulating a spaceship docking operation, for example, the user had virtual tools and could carry out docking tasks with them.

Before I chronicle further developments, let me mention one of the interesting precursors to Sutherland's work—Sensorama, created by Morton Heilig. Heilig drew his inspiration from the possibility of extending the experience of the cinema to all the senses. Thus, in the 1950s, he developed a machine that looked like an arcade entertainment booth and gave the user the impression of being immersed in

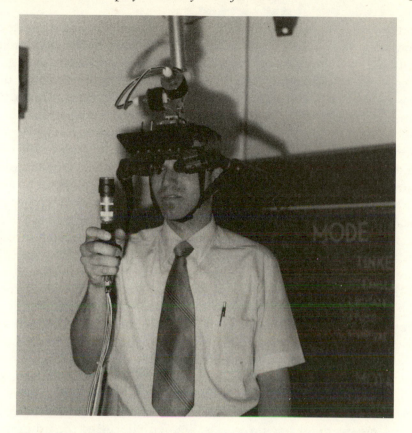

Figure 2.1   The first computer-generated, head-mounted, and interactive display, developed by Ivan Sutherland (courtesy of the University of Utah and the Evans & Sutherland Computer Corporation).

another world. Heilig's machine not only projected cinematic images of an environment on a screen in front of the user but also provided, among other things, the sensation of the smell of the environment by having the machine emit certain scents at the appropriate moments during the Sensorama experience (Heilig 1992; Rheingold 1991:49–60). Heilig believed, incidentally, that immersive cinema should take into account the fact that "each sense monopolizes man's attention in the following proportions: sight 70 percent, hearing 20 percent, smell 5 percent, touch 4 percent, taste 1 percent" (1992:285). It will be interesting to bear these figures in mind when we come to examine present-day VR systems.[3]

Nevertheless, this device, like Sutherland's, failed to take off at the time. In the case of Sutherland's "ultimate display," the failure resulted from limitations on the computing power that was available for handling the complex computer graphics and the interaction. In hindsight, we can also say that computers needed to become much more widespread and diverse before ideas about using them for purposes other than calculating could take root. Thus, more than two decades passed before fully fledged VR systems emerged. As Biocca has pointed out, VR does not consist of one technology but of several (1992a:10), and hence it took years of advances in a variety of fields before powerful VR systems could be put together. But although Sutherland's ideas and his devices have subsequently come to be associated with the origins of VR, a number of other developments—from Sutherland's work onward—eventually led to the take-off of VR technology in the late 1980s. These developments occurred in three areas: art, flight simulation and robotics, and military and space-related research.

In art, the first person to explore the potential of VR-like interactive computing devices was Myron Krueger, although he prefers the label "artificial reality" (Krueger 1991). In the early 1970s, Krueger created a gallery installation that allowed users to interact with a two-dimensional computer-generated environment. The difference between Krueger's "artificial reality" and immersive virtual reality systems is that he is not attempting to create a simulation that gives the user the impression of bodily "presence" inside a virtual world. Instead, Krueger's system projects a silhouette image of the user onto a wall-sized screen so that the user can interact with these two-dimensional "worlds." Interactivity is achieved by recording the user's movements with a video camera and using the computer to correlate the image of the user with the features of the "world." As this system makes use of an image of the participant's body rather than providing an immersive experience, it has also become known as a "mirror-world" (Vincent and Wyshinski 1994). The system also has a feature that allows several users to interact with one another in the projected screen "world."

Compared with Sutherland's system, Krueger's "artificial reality" is mainly aimed at exploring the expressive or creative potential of interacting with computers. It is noteworthy that Krueger's systems have only recently, since the take-off of VR, received significant attention. This despite the fact that his systems did not face the same technical hurdles Sutherland's did, and again, despite the fact that Krueger's installations clearly constituted a departure in the use of computing in art. We can also anticipate more recent developments here by noting that although Krueger has continued to exhibit his interactive work, including more flexible and imaginative devices and worlds, his artificial reality systems have not become widespread—although they are inexpensive compared with immersive VR systems and demand much less computing power.[4] Krueger's work, then, is one of the conceptions of the technology that has not become widespread, although, again, it needs to be pointed out that his device is not, strictly speaking, VR, as "artificial reality" does not give the user a sense of "presence" or immersion in a three-dimensional world. Nevertheless, Krueger's concept of interacting with computer-generated worlds has been an important influence on the development of VR-like devices in the arts.[5]

Flight simulators and robotics have also contributed to VR, particularly with regard to human factors issues. Flight simulators and other types of vehicle simulation have been developed since the 1960s, mainly for training purposes (Vince 1992). Inasmuch as there have been attempts to think about the psychological issues in VR—particularly motion sickness—research on simulator sickness has provided a body of knowledge to draw on.[6] Much of the research on human factors relating to VR, therefore, refers back to earlier simulator research. The same is true of research on robotics or teleoperations. The use of robot arms, for example, overlaps with VR issues such as the input of the user's commands and conveying the machines' operations back to the user (Durlach and Mavor 1995:304–361).

The area of flight simulation has been dominated by research conducted by the United States Air Force and by NASA, to which we shall turn in a moment. Before we do so, it should be noted that vehicle simulation and robotics research have to a large extent been driven by considerations of cost and safety. Operating expensive vehicles or using machinery in dangerous or hazardous environments provides a strong incentive for using simulation and telepresence. Hence, too, there is an interest today in using VR for applications in areas in which simulation previously might have been used. The pragmatic advantages of simulation also deserve to be emphasized because military simulation and VR are often associated and VR is thus thought to have sinister implications. It is worth keeping in mind, though, that virtual battlefields systems such as SIMNET (which will be described later) are used, as far as I am aware, for training purposes only and therefore play mainly an indirect role in military operations.[7] This is also a good point at which to highlight the difference between simulation and VR—simulation makes the user feel present in a vehicle (or similar), whereas VR allows the user to experience the environment directly.[8]

Although there has been much work on simulation for military uses, more recently, in the 1990s, the main influence of military work on VR has been in the area of networked VR. The military research that was more directly linked to VR before the recent take-off of VR technology was the work on head-mounted displays carried out for the air force and for NASA. Two research sites are particularly important here: one is Wright-Patterson Air Force Base near Dayton, Ohio, where flight simulation has been ongoing since the 1960s and so-called head-up displays (i.e., augmented reality) have been developed for pilots. The other is NASA Ames Research Center in Mountain View, California, where research has focused, again, on head-mounted displays, partly with a view to carrying out remote operations in space. It was at NASA in the mid-1980s that the first head-mounted display was built using off-the-shelf (that is, commercially available) pocket television screens. The idea was that these inexpensive screens would be used to generate or display a remote environment (as opposed to using them to display flight instruments, which had been a common feature of pilot helmets). The use of a display device with these screens was a radical departure from the high-powered and expensive flight helmets that had been under development at Wright-Patterson and elsewhere (Kalawsky 1993:117–118). Another center of VR research that can be mentioned briefly (it will be discussed more fully in the next chapter) is the computer science department at the University of North Carolina at Chapel Hill, which early on played a particularly important role in developing force-feedback displays that the user could manipulate with a mechanical arm. Ideas and trials for a computer-generated virtual environment were being pursued at Chapel Hill in the late 1980s (Brooks 1988).

The Technology Takes Off

A number of other research centers and innovations also played a role in setting the scene for VR, but we have at least touched on the major ones.[9] The extent to which these sources influenced the take-off of VR technology in the late 1980s is difficult to assess. A number of those who developed VR systems in the 1980s were partly aware of research Sutherland and others had carried out, but it is difficult to reconstruct the links between the various individuals involved during this period. One thing is certain: apart from Jonathan Waldern's parallel research in the United Kingdom (which we shall encounter in Chapter 4), VR development in the late 1980s and early 1990s was concentrated in Silicon Valley. Jaron Lanier in particular was working closely with NASA researchers in Mountain View (Rheingold 1991:154–174). It should also be mentioned that a number of those who worked on the early VR systems came from the completely different area of computer games and particularly from the firm Atari. In fact, many people who were involved in the computer industry in Silicon Valley in the 1980s got their start during the profitable boom in computer games that took place around 1980.

Apart from this similarity in background and the geographical concentration of the personnel, an important precondition for the take-off of VR was the rapid increase in performance and declining cost of computers in the 1980s.[10] These were two crucial requirements, particularly for computer graphics machines capable of generating a "realistic" three-dimensional world. Computer processing power grew rapidly as a result of the expansion of the market for personal computers, and this also led to other important innovations, especially sophisticated methods for human-computer interaction tied to the advent of the mouse and the use of icons. Thus, whereas the conceptual groundwork had been laid much earlier by Sutherland, it was only during the 1980s that the technical means became available to produce systems that were more than prototypes.

In the late 1980s, Jaron Lanier was the first to start attaching the label "virtual reality" to interactive computer-generated three-dimensional immersive displays. With several collaborators, he put together the first fully immersive system of the type that has since come to be widely identified with VR: head-mounted display, bodysuit, and glove. This became the first commercially available VR system and was soon followed by an innovative system in which two users could jointly experience the same environment, Reality Built For Two or RB2. The story of how these early VR systems were put together by tinkering with and cobbling together various artifacts in a garage (or in this case, in a living room) and how this amateur effort rapidly became a successful company (VPL) that developed VR systems for commercial customers has all the hallmarks of the typical—if often somewhat mythologized—story of the emergence of new technologies. Even the denouement of the story, in which Lanier grew tired of and withdrew from the commercial aspect of VR and was eventually ousted from the company he founded, has a familiar ring.[11]

This sequence of events is comparable to the pattern followed in the creation of other new technologies. What is remarkable (although not unique) in this case is the "lull" of more than 20 years between Sutherland's ideas and the take-off phase of VR, on the one hand, and the speed with which this technology, once it had received the label "virtual reality," generated an enormous amount of interest, on the other. Since the early 1990s, research and development efforts have mushroomed so that there are now dozens of institutions devoted to VR research. Within a few years, VR has become a multimillion-dollar industry.

After the lull, it took VR only a few years to move from obscurity to becoming a well-known technology that is being pursued with the same amount of energy and interest as many of the more well-established technologies. One point that emerges even from this cursory account of the factors that came together in the making of VR is that the pattern of VR development has been uneven and its sources diverse. Thus the past trajectory of this technology may not give a reliable indication about the direction in which it is heading.

At this stage we can return to some of the issues raised earlier about the sociology of science and technology. In Chapter 1, I argued that the preconditions of scientific and technological advancement can only be described in general terms and that with such an account, it then becomes important to concentrate on the social implications of this advance. Before we examine those implications, it is important to summarize how the advances in VR technology have come about.

The first point in this regard is that as with many other technologies, particularly in the twentieth century, scientific and technological advances have gone hand in hand. Hence, it is only possible to specify after the event which particular scientific and technological advances were required before virtual reality could take off. Among these, again, were computer processing power, high-resolution visual displays, and ideas about interacting with computer displays. The computing power for Sutherland's "ultimate display"—its black-and-white wire frame image, its display resolution, and its mechanical tracking—were all modest compared with the performance of Lanier's Reality Built For Two system (Kalawsky 1993:20–22,

210–220) and other systems of the mid- to late 1980s. Yet in terms of ideas, Lanier and others were only refining and building upon Sutherland's notion of an interactive computer-generated world.

Secondly, it is difficult to assess the role played by Lanier's evocative term "virtual reality." The same idea is conveyed by Sutherland's "ultimate display," but it is hard to see how this term, or Sutherland's black-and-white wire frame images, could have fired the imagination in the same way that Lanier's RB2 did a little over two decades later. As we shall see, Lanier's in some ways misleading term (users are not experiencing reality but rather an environment other than the one in which they are physically present) has also led to confused expectations surrounding the technology. Still, by comparison with the "ultimate display," Lanier's technology had, as a result of advances in the intervening years, moved many steps closer to creating the kinds of VR systems that we are familiar with today.

This brief history of early VR systems allows us to be more precise in defining VR technology: virtual reality is a computer-generated display that allows or compels the user (or users) to have a feeling of being present in an environment other than the one that they are actually in and to interact with that environment (Ellis, 1991:324; Sheridan, 1992:274). As we shall see, there will be instances in which it may be difficult to differentiate VR from kindred technologies or to gauge whether some systems that have been labeled VR should in fact be counted as such. Still, this definition is workable in the sense that it sets VR apart from other technologies and identifies its key features.

An Overview of Virtual Reality Technology

We can now examine the main technical features of VR systems. The aim cannot be to provide a comprehensive survey of current research on VR, since the field is now vast and rapidly changing.[12] This survey also cannot be exhaustive in terms of including the many manufacturers of VR systems and components. Such completeness is not necessary since, as we shall see, some areas are much more central to VR development than others. What is important is to get a sense of the range of technological capabilities of the various kinds of systems and devices. This will allow us to see why particular technologies are used in certain settings and to gauge the reasons for the popularity of the technologies and the manner of their application. This overview will also allow us to get a sense of how the range of devices and systems is being narrowed or widened, which is always a key question for a "new technology at the outset" (Dierkes and Hoffman 1992).

It should be mentioned before we proceed that it is difficult to disentangle VR from related areas of research. As we have just seen, there have been several sources for VR technology, among them Sutherland's computer display devices, military head-mounted displays for aircraft, and aircraft simulators. All of these devices have made different contributions to the technology: Sutherland's work led to new ways of thinking about human-computer interaction, head-mounted displays yielded high-powered optics, and simulators provided a reservoir of knowledge about human factors.

Of course, even this picture is simplified. Research on VR has been intertwined with other areas. Other fields of research, such as robotics or projects that involve human-machine interaction like the "movie map" project (Brand 1987:141)—which allowed users to navigate around the videorecorded streets and houses of Aspen, Colorado— have also intersected with virtual environments research, providing an additional reason to limit this overview. Still, by the time the first helmet-and-glove VR systems emerged in the late 1980s, there already existed a range of devices and techniques, including Lanier's RB2, which Kalawsky describes as the "first complete virtual environment system to become [commercially] available" (1993:210). The point at which the technology came out of the lab and into the public domain is perhaps a good indication of what separates the phase of research on prototypes from that of the social career of a technological artifact.

Virtual reality systems consist of three parts: the devices that display the virtual world to the user (the output of the computer); the devices that enter the state of the human operator into the computer (the input into the computer); and the computer hardware and software that generate the virtual environment and provide the link between input and output. We shall take each of these in turn. But as this overview is heavily biased toward certain devices, it is necessary to say something about how this bias is justified by means of anticipating the conclusion: namely, that certain technological components have become key reverse salients or bottlenecks in VR.[13] Foremost among these bottlenecks are visual display resolution, position tracking "lag," the computer hardware and software for generating virtual worlds, and, of course, cost. This means that more attention will be paid, for example, to the visual rather than the auditory channel, or to position-tracking as opposed to force-feedback devices.

Output—Visual Displays

The head-mounted display (HMD), which displays the image of the virtual environment or world to the user, has become the most distinctive feature of VR systems.[14] The image of people wearing devices that look like helmets or glasses has become closely associated with VR, even though there are various other options for displaying a computer-generated environment, such as displaying the image on a wall-size screen that surrounds a user who wears 3-D glasses or using a laser to scan images directly onto the viewer's retina. Here we shall concentrate on HMDs, as these have become the most widely used VR devices.

Sutherland's mechanically head-coupled, monochromatic displays in the 1960s featured line drawings displayed on two small cathode-ray tubes (CRTs) with a "spot size" (the equivalent of what today is called a "pixel" or picture element) of .6 mm (Kalawsky 1993:21). The most advanced displays today, which for the most part still use CRTs or liquid crystal displays (LCDs), feature over a million pixels per square inch in monochromatic mode. The increase in resolution from Sutherland's displays to those that are used today is thus one of several orders of magnitude, and it means that whereas Sutherland's display could only represent objects in outline, current HMDs are closer in quality to television images. The VPL Eyephone for the RB2 represented an enormous leap in the quality of resolution with 25,715 pixels per eye (Kalawsky 1993:118), but at the time, this HMD, which was the only one commercially available in 1991, cost approximately $10,000. Several comparable HMDs have recently come onto the market priced $1,000 or less.

One figure that has often been cited with respect to "visual reality"—the point at which the human eye will be unable to distinguish between a real image and an artificial one—is "80 million polygons per picture." However, since the VR image needs to be updated to represent a changing virtual environment, "if we wish photorealistic VE's at 10 frames/second, this translates into 800 million polygons/second" (Durlach and Mavor 1995:252; cf. Rheingold 1991:168). This display resolution may seem a distant goal and it is regarded as such by researchers, but it needs to be placed in context, given that some commercial VR graphics processors, such as UNC's Pixel-Planes, are capable of delivering several million polygons per second and that a number of the more expensive commercial HMD displays (those that cost over $50,000) are capable of image resolution of several hundred thousand pixels (Biocca and Delaney 1995:69).[15] Military HMD technology is capable of higher resolutions at a price of over half a million dollars (Durlach and Mavor 1995:124), but even the HMDs that are consumer products, priced under $1,000, are capable of almost television-like resolutions of 200x200 or 40,000 pixels.[16] It needs to be added that visual display technology is an area in which there is intense competition to develop more powerful devices, not only for VR but also for high-definition television and computer screens.

In addition to display resolution, there are a number of other features of the visual display that are important for the user. Among these are the field of view, the effect of a slightly different interpupillary distance of human beings (many displays now allow this distance to be adjusted by the user), the brightness (or luminescence) of the display, the degree of overlap between the two images to create a stereoscopic effect (binocular overlap), and a number of others. Perhaps equally important from the point of view of the human operator is the comfort of HMDs: many existing HMDs are heavy and the lighter ones tend to be less powerful. Nevertheless, several HMDs now weigh about one pound or less, a relatively comfortable weight; that is, these are devices that can be worn for some time without muscular strain.

It should also be mentioned that there are various other tools for displaying virtual worlds. For example, visual displays do not necessarily block out the real world. Some, like Sutherland's "ultimate display," allow the user to see the real world at the same time. These displays have been labeled "augmented reality" since they superimpose the image of the virtual environment onto the real one. This superimposition is particularly useful in training and scientific visualization applications. Still other displays are projected onto large screens that envelop the user, such as the so-called CAVE system, which has been used, for example, in vehicle simulations (Cruz-Neira, Sandin, and DeFanti 1993; Durlach and Mavor 1995:428, 442). Another means of displaying an immersive three-dimensional image to the user is by means of a boom-mounted display (such as the Fakespace BOOM or

Binocular Omni-Orientation Monitor), which the user holds to the eye instead of wearing a head-mounted display. At the HITLab, which we will return to in the next chapter, researchers are working on ways to scan the image directly onto the retina with a laser display. There is also a question about whether a 3-D environment displayed on a (2-D) computer screen or "desktop" VR, sometimes in connection with 3-D glasses, should be considered (immersive) virtual reality—but this is an issue we shall come back to.

In any case, the most common form of VR is the LCD or CRT head-mounted stereoscopic display. Despite a number of possible options, visual displays seem to have congealed around this technology for the time being. The trade-offs in this area are between cost and fidelity of the image, and although the technology is making rapid advances, high-end and consumer-oriented devices are entering a stage of intense commercial competition. A recent product survey listed over 40 commercially available HMDs, divided more or less evenly between products for the high-end professional market and the low-end consumer market.[17]

Before we move on, we can summarize the advances in this area in nontechnical terms by saying that computer-generated displays of virtual environments have gone from black-and-white line drawings, via the cartoonlike images of Lanier's system, to highly "realistic" images. It should also be mentioned that apart from the technical term HMD, VR displays have also been called "helmets." More recently, because HMDs have become lighter and are shaped more like eyeglasses, the term VR "glasses" has become more widespread (see Figure 2.2). Since VR "glasses" are more comfortable, this form of the technology is currently in the ascendant.

Output—Auditory Displays

Auditory output provides the user with the impression that sound is coming from a three-dimensional source. The device that is typically used for producing this kind of sound is a set of stereophonic headphones that are attached to the HMD. The hardware required for producing an auditory virtual environment is a sound "card" that slots into the computer system. One particular device, the Convolvotron by Crystal River Engineering, originally developed in collaboration with NASA Ames, has dominated this field. It has been used in many popular VR systems, such as the early VPL systems and

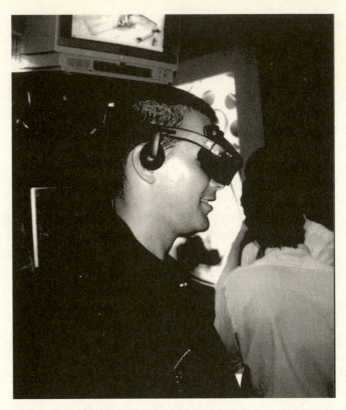

Figure 2.2   The Virtual I/O "i-glasses," one of a number of recent HMDs aimed at the consumer market.

those currently produced by Division. The Convolvotron is based on calculations that have been made about the way in which sound from different directions and different distances arrive at the right and left ear of the user at slightly different times.[18] The position of the user then needs to be related to the auditory environment that is being produced to create the impression of a realistic environment.

Although the fidelity of 3-D sound has been the subject of some discussion, the issue has been far outweighed by others such as image display resolution and position-tracking accuracy. As we shall see, this has much to do with the fact that VR systems are so strongly visually oriented, but it may also be that the capacity of existing sound devices to create the impression of a three-dimensional environment does not need to be greatly enhanced in order to be acceptable to users, unlike the fidelity of three-dimensional graphics.

Thus, the authors of the National Research Council study, which tried to outline research needs in VR technology, concluded that "with one major exception . . . the technology for the auditory channel is either adequate now or will be adequate in the near future," the exception being "acoustic environments with complex, realistic room reflections" (Durlach and Mavor 1995:159, 160). A related point is that whereas in 1991, the Convolvotron system, which could be used to create and play back 3-D environments, cost tens of thousands of dollars, current versions of these systems cost less than $1,000. It can also be noted that many VR entertainment systems use the stereophonic headphones that are mounted on the HMD for producing sound like music and voice narration (i.e., sound that is not located in the virtual environment) rather than for generating a full 3-D auditory environment.

Input—Position Tracking

Position-trackers relay the user's bodily movements to the computer and thus allow the user to interact with the virtual environment. The most straightforward way to input the user's head movements is by means of a mechanical arm. As we have seen, this was Sutherland's initial method, and there was no significant lag in his system between the user's movements and the computer's response. For this reason, a mechanical link is still used in some systems, like the Fakespace BOOM, although such a device has the drawback that the user's hands are not free since they must guide the display device (alternatively, this type of display can be strapped to the operator's head, but in this case, although the hands are free, the user's head must guide the counterbalanced boom-type arm; see Figures 2.3 and 2.4).

Other trackers can be divided into optical, magnetic, and acoustic devices.[19] These can be used to track the head, the hands, or the whole body. In most cases, the sensors are located on the HMD, the hand-held device or glove and sometimes the user's body. But there are also systems in which the sensors are located, for example, in a room-size space. In that case, emitters on the user's body relay the user's position to the VR system. There is also a difference between trackers that require a tangible link between the user and the system (i.e., a set of wires) and those in which the signal between user and system is immaterial (i.e., light or sound waves).[20] But although a variety of technical options are being pursued in research labs, the most widespread option is to locate the sensors on the HMD, glove, or hand-held 3-D mouse, and in some cases other parts of the body, and to link them with

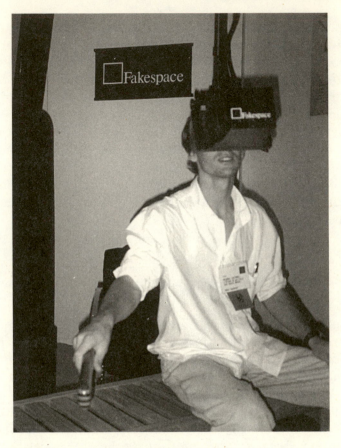

Figure 2.3   The Fakespace BOOM with sailboat tiller.

wires.[21] Again, this is an example of the way in which the technology has congealed around one particular type of artifact.

An additional point about position-tracking is that apart from the degree of fidelity, from the user's point of view, much depends on the physical makeup of this device. What, for example, should be the length of the set of wires that connect the HMD and glove to the computer? Or again, how far can the user move before position-tracking devices lose their accuracy? With magnetic trackers, the space within which the user can move is typically a few feet or less. Most trackers are also subject to interference—in the case of magnetic sensors, for example, from metallic objects. Alternatively, in the case of systems that track the user's movement in a room-size space without a physical link between the user and the system, the size of the room, to paraphrase Wittgenstein, is the limit of the user's world. Or again,

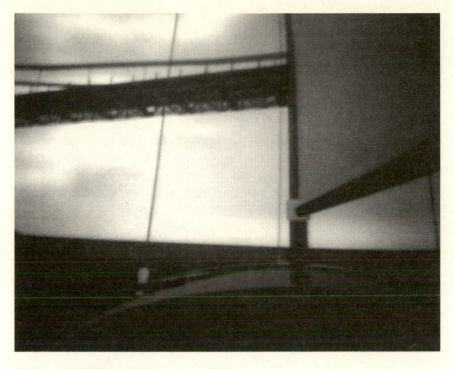

Figure 2.4   Sailboat passing under a bridge.

with the Fakespace BOOM, the user's movement is limited by the range of the mechanical arm. The fidelity requirements of position-tracking devices also vary with the applications, so that a VR system for surgical training, for example, needs to be more accurate than an architectural model. In any case, we should keep in mind that tracking devices physically limit the user's movement.

The main reason tracking devices are crucial to VR development, apart from providing "freedom" for the user, is that the lag between the user's movements and the system's response is possibly the most important factor in relation to what—apart from eyestrain—may be the key health and safety aspect of VR; namely "simulator" sickness. We shall return to this issue later. In this context, however, it is interesting to note that whereas differences in visual display resolution between high-end and low-end systems will be readily apparent to anyone who is familiar with a number of VR systems, for the layperson it is often difficult to notice differences in lag between systems with quite different specifications.

Finally, the term "lag" is a simplification, since, technically, this phenomenon is composed of a number of issues pertaining to human factors and relates not only to position-tracking but to a number of components of VR systems (Kalawsky 1993:277–291). For our purposes, the following summary of the state of the technology that incorporates the main aspects of position-tracking is sufficient: "Current systems have adequate levels of resolution (the smallest change a system can detect) and accuracy (the range within which the reported position is correct)," but they are "often plagued by lags, the time between the moment a user makes a movement and the moment the computer responds to the movement. Part of this lag is attributable to the slowness of the position-tracker and part is due to the time required to process the location information by the host computer" (Biocca and Delaney 1995:100).

The most popular position-tracking products are the magnetic trackers made by Polhemus and Ascension Technology, which achieve latencies (the rate at which new data can be acquired) of around 20–30 milliseconds (Durlach and Mavor 1995:193). This is not far off from the 10 milliseconds that the National Research Council study postulates as an acceptable standard for high-performance head-tracking, but it needs to be added here that "accuracy requirements are very application dependent" (Durlach and Mavor 1995:190). We should also note that the Polhemus position-tracker for the VPL RB2 in 1991 cost more than $2,500, whereas some devices today cost less than $1,000.

Inputting the Body

Most VR systems use sensors to record the user's head and hand movements. Apart from the HMD, the most widespread means for inputting movement of the hand are the data glove or hand-held devices with push buttons. It is interesting that whereas most of the earlier VR systems featured gloves, today hand-held devices are much more common. This trend has little to do with technical constraints—glove technology is relatively advanced, reliable, and inexpensive. But it may be that joysticklike hand-held devices represent an easier means for the operator to navigate and undertake other simple tasks in the virtual world, and moving through the virtual world is often the main purpose of manual input.

Hence, although gloves are used in a small number of professional VR applications, most VR systems use hand-held or "flying" 3-D mice, deskbound joysticks or spaceballs.[22] Most of these hand-operated devices have buttons for the input of additional commands like picking up objects or, in games, shooting things. A variety of such devices are commercially available and many are aimed at the consumer market. They often cost less than $1,000 and in some cases less than $100.

A fully immersive and interactive VR system would, of course, allow input from the user's whole body. But again, whereas bodysuits (or datasuits), featured prominently in early VR systems such as VPL's RB2, today, among researchers and developers, the bodysuit has become almost extinct. (The interesting exceptions are media representations of the technology, which may be lagging behind technological developments in this respect.) Research is still being devoted to other bodily input devices such as exoskeletons, which can also be seen as output or display devices, since they provide force-feedback to the user (of which more in a moment), devices for recognizing facial expressions and eye movements, and those that use psychophysiological input like blood pressure and brain waves (electroencephalography). None of these devices have become part of mainstream VR research, however, and they are only used for specialized applications such as telerobotics for hazardous environments or medicine. Some researchers also include voice-recognition systems as part of VR technology, since this constitutes a means of interacting with—or more precisely, entering commands into—the computer.[23] But if the focus of VR technology is on "presence" and sensory (as opposed to intellectual) interaction with the virtual world, then voice recognition, which is still very difficult to achieve with existing computing technology, is not part of VR technology. Voice input, in the form of a microphone that enables the operator to communicate with others in multiparticipant virtual worlds, however, is technologically very simple.[24] This type of microphone is featured in many multiuser VR systems, including the Virtuality arcade entertainment game.

Output to the Body

Similar considerations apply to the devices that are used to display information other than images and sound to the body. Exoskeletons that provide force-feedback have already been mentioned, but there are also devices for the olfactory (smell) and gustatory (taste) channels, for the receptors on the skin and other tactile sensations, and for conveying a sense of movement to the body by means of motion platforms, treadmills, and the like. Research is ongoing in all of these areas and surveys of VR typically review these devices. Yet these devices, again, are expensive prototypes mainly used in specialist fields. The main exception is motion platforms, which are widely used in training and entertainment applications. One difference between these two areas of application is that whereas training requires realistic simulations of motion, entertainment systems are often designed to create an exaggerated sense of motion. In any case, most motion platforms and similar devices do not provide a sense of being in a virtual world but rather of being in a vehicle. For this reason, and because the technology is well established, they have not appeared very much in VR research laboratories and the refinement of these devices has been undertaken mainly by those who manufacture VR systems for specific applications.

A related issue is that of the representation of the user's body in the virtual world. In the context of output to the body (but this also applies to bodily input), it should be mentioned that the vast majority of systems feature a body that consists of a computer-generated image related to the position of the user's head and hand, which means that output to the body—as well as input apart from head and arm movement—are to a large extent irrelevant. The representation of the user's body is an important issue and it will be discussed in detail in the next chapter. In the meantime, we can note again that the technology has congealed around certain devices, and although this is related to a number of factors, it should be mentioned in passing that the devices that have become most prevalent are those that are similar to the model provided by Sutherland's original device and that fit his vision of future systems, which concentrated on visual output (1965:507).[25]

Computer Hardware

The first interactive computer-generated environments that were devised by Sutherland were powered by TX-2 and Digital Equipment Corporation PDP-10 computers (Rheingold 1991:109–110), room-size machines that cost several million dollars and had a fraction of the capabilities of today's personal computers. The hardware for the VPL RB2 was a specially designed computer that also required an additional high-performance computer graphics workstation of the type that was available commercially at the time. The computer hardware needed for a single user of VPL's RB2 thus cost more than $75,000. For two users, more powerful workstations were necessary and this pushed the cost to $250,000 (Rheingold 1991:166).

The computer technology for VR systems needs to do three things: manage the input and output devices, generate and update the virtual environment, and provide a link between the devices and the virtual environment (cf. Durlach and Mavor 1995:248). But whereas some VR systems (such as Division's) use a custom-made hardware architecture to configure these functionalities, many of today's systems are based on high-performance computer graphics workstations (like those produced by Silicon Graphics) or high-end personal computers to which a special graphics board has been added. The distinction between the last two is diminishing, as the hardware from high-end graphics workstations is being incorporated within consumer products like personal computers and computer games. Put the other way around, the personal computer has become comparable in price and performance to the computer graphics workstations formerly limited to professional uses.

At the high end, as mentioned earlier, specialized computer hardware for VR, like that which is being developed at the University of North Carolina, Silicon Graphics, and Evans & Sutherland, is capable of generating up to a million polygons per second (Durlach and Mavor 1995:299–303). Common commercial computer graphics workstations used for VR, like those made by Silicon Graphics, are advertised as being able to process more than two million polygons per second, yet as the authors of the National Research Council study point out, a realistic assessment of the kind of virtual world that can be represented with this kind of system is "7500 textured polygons at 30 frames/s," which, they add, "is not a very detailed world" (Durlach and Mavor 1995:269). A VR system based on a personal computer like that which powers the Virtuality arcade games or similar IBM compatible personal computers with graphics boards, by comparison, can render a few hundred textured polygons running at roughly half the speed (Durlach and Mavor 1995:261). It needs to be added that—just as in the case of visual display devices—there has been intense competition to achieve higher computer graphics capabilities within the consumer electronics market. This competition is partly driven by the logic that computers are generally used much more for generating and manipulating images as opposed to storing and processing words and numbers. Thus graphics workstations, which were the most expensive components of VPL's VR systems, have doubled their power several times since around 1990 (Durlach and Mavor 1995:301) and the performance that was available then at around $100,000 is now contained in machines that cost less than $10,000.

Computer Software

At the time of Sutherland's first HMD, the distinction between hardware and software was practically nonexistent. Similarly, the field of computer graphics was still in its infancy.[26] By the time of VPL's RB2, the software for this system featured a world-modeling package (Swivel) with which virtual worlds could be built on the computer, as well as Body Electric software that allowed the user to build virtual worlds from within the virtual world. The latter was one of the most novel features of VR systems when they first appeared, but as we shall see, it has since become less prominent. As Kalawsky points out, "at the moment, modeling tools for virtual environment applications are designed to be used outside the virtual environment" (Kalawsky 1993:249); that is, most virtual worlds are designed on a desktop computer and the user can manipulate the virtual world from within only to a limited extent (i.e., picking up objects, as opposed to creating them). This is a point we shall come back to.

The main functions of VR software are to generate the virtual world, to enable interaction, and to link the various components of the system. There are currently dozens of VR software packages or "toolkits." Some are available for free as "shareware" from universities, like VEOS from the HITLab and Minimal Reality from the University of Alberta. The majority, however, are marketed commercially and range in cost from several hundred to tens of thousands of dollars. Some VR software has been developed for specific applications and is not in the public domain, like the software for networked military simulations or for some professional uses.

There is also a fundamental divide between software that runs on workstations like Silicon Graphics, typically for use with the UNIX operating system, and that which can run on personal computers based on Windows, DOS, and Macintosh. Perhaps even more important from the user's point of view is whether the world-modeling software is designed to be operated by professional developers or by the end user. Software for high-end systems tends to be designed for developers; that is, it requires further programming to fit particular applications. Software for personal computers, however, is often designed for end users.

Like the other main components of VR systems, software performance has steadily improved and the cost has dropped sharply. This is what one might expect in the light of patterns in the computer industry generally. The software for VPL's RB2 cost approximately $10,000, whereas today commercial VR software packages are sometimes priced below $1,000. There has also been a trend away from software for the developer market and an increase in software aimed at the consumer or end-user market.

If we combine the advances in the hardware of computer workstations for VR with the platform independence of most current VR software packages, it is clear that this has become an area of intense commercial competition. Because of the competitive market, calls for software standards (Kalawasky 1993:247; Durlach and Mavor 1995:291) are unlikely to be heeded; or, if there are any standard-setters, they are likely to be determined by market share, as in other areas of computing.

The question about compatibility between different packages is particularly important in VR since, as Kalawsky notes, "modeling of objects will probably remain the most time consuming task, hence, the most expensive" (1993: 249). For this reason, some software firms have adopted the strategy of providing large "libraries" of virtual objects that can be converted (or "ported") from one VR system to another.[27]

Similarly, a number of firms have begun to specialize in "clip art," or ready-made 3-D computer graphics objects, in the first instance for computer-aided design but latterly also for VR. In other words, a key aim of VR software developers has been to try to become the vendor of the most commonly used real estate in the virtual world. It needs to be added that the success of this strategy is related to two issues: one is the degree to which virtual worlds can be created from the inside or by end users, and the other is the degree to which three-dimensional objects can be "captured" by means of photography or other sensing devices and imported into virtual worlds (Biocca and

Delaney 1995:112). Both are possible with existing technologies, although the latter is in its technological infancy and still prohibitive in cost.

Networked VR

VPL's RB2 was the first multiparticipant or multiuser VR system, though the Virtuality arcade game, which allowed up to four players to share the same virtual world, followed not long after, in 1991. To put these developments into context, prior to the introduction of consumer VR systems that enabled more than one user to participate, the American Department of Defense produced networked tank and aircraft simulators (SIMNET or SIMulator NETwork) to enable over 300 people to participate in simulated combat via networked capsules with 2–D screens and 3-D computer-generated environments in the late 1980s (Katz 1994:110; U.S. Congress, Office of Technology Assessment 1994). Another useful point of reference is the networked game Habitat that allowed hundreds of participants to move around together in a world on a 2-D computer screen and interact as cartoon figures. In Habitat, players communicate with each other with speech bubble messages and the networking takes place via the telephone system on a pay-per-play basis (Morningstar and Farmer 1991).

Networked VR systems can be divided into those that are specifically employed to support a small number of VR systems (local area networks) and larger networks that support generic telecommunications or data transfer (wide area networks). The former typically rely on ethernet links that operate at 10 megabits per second, which is fast enough for existing types of multiparticipant VR systems.[28] Links within supercomputer centers, to give an example of a different type of local area network, are supported by means of special fiber optic cable at 100 megabits/second (Durlach and Mavor 1995:366). Existing wide area networks, by comparison, have only modest bandwidths. Telephony services, for example, require bandwidths of 64 kilobits/second or between 32 and 16 kilobits/second in a compressed state (Stallings and van Slyke 1994).

The most high-speed long-distance VR network to date has followed the distributed interactive simulation (DIS) standard set by the Department of Defense for networked simulations (Moshell et al. 1995; Stytz et al. 1995). Under this standard, which is the successor of SIMNET, the Naval Postgraduate School Networked Vehicle Simulator (NPSNET) was used by multiple participants in a handful of locations across the United States and carried by ethernet and a dedicated T1 (1.5 megabit/second) link (Zyda et al. 1993; Macedonia et al. 1994). The fidelity of this shared virtual environment, which runs on Silicon Graphics workstations and supports the use of HMDs, over such a wide area network depends to a large extent on the complexity of the world and of the interactions, but the NPSNET link is comparable to virtual worlds produced on other high-end VR systems. It should be mentioned that in this type of long-distance link, there is a lag of 300 milliseconds, for example, for data transfer across the United States (Durlach and Mavor 1995:371), which is a barrier to effective interaction. Also, it has often been pointed out that the speed of light ultimately provides another impediment to long-distance links of this type. A final barrier to networked VR of a different type is cost. T1 lines, for example, "with installation expenses of $40,000 and operating costs of $140,000 per year" (Durlach and Mavor 1995:372), are out of the reach of all but a few institutions with university or military backing.

The authors of the National Research Council report conclude that "like the Department of Defense, the video game industry is not interested in generalizability of information transfer, nor is it interested in openness and accessibility. The danger is that the video game industry will set the networking protocol standards at the low end and the Defense/DIS community will set the standards at the high end. Neither of these standards is general enough for the widespread application development we would like to see" (Durlach and Mavor 1995:372). This view may be too narrow. There has been some interest, for example, in using military network standards for networked entertainment purposes (Katz 1994). Recently, moreover, virtual worlds produced by VRML (Virtual Reality Modeling Language) have been introduced on the Internet, and trials are under way for virtual shopping on British Telecom's telephone system. There are also various high bandwidth networked VR trials in academic and commercial research environments, like VIRTUOSI (Benford 1994). Hence the standard that defines the scope and the technical quality of networked virtual worlds could be set at a number of levels. At this point, however, we are moving away from issues that relate to VR and entering the domain of telecommunications technology. And although the future of networked VR depends on this technology, one major difference between networked and current VR systems is that the latter are still mainly stand-alone technology. In comparison, telecommunications technology can be seen as a "large technological system," to borrow Hughes's (1987) terminology, and it is therefore shaped by forces that are quite different from those that shape VR technology.

Looking Back and Looking Forward

In the context of this overview of the technology, it is important to return to the question of how technology and social life are interrelated. It will be apparent at this point that VR technology has congealed into particular combinations of devices. Thus, scientific and technological advance in VR systems has come to crystallize around a small number of reverse salients: visual display resolution, position-tracking, and computer processing power—especially for computer graphics. We can add as a fourth possible reverse salient the bandwidth for wide area VR networks. Two of these, position-tracking and network bandwidth, are more applications-specific than the others, because position-tracking relates closely to the accuracy of the task and networking depends on the number of users and the complexity of the communication. The other two reverse salients are less closely related to specific applications, but they have also been subject to an intense technological push. And finally, all these obstacles are interrelated: there is little point in being able to generate a virtual environment that cannot be displayed adequately or that does not respond adequately to the user, and vice versa. Similarly, high-fidelity environments are useless if the network is unable to carry them.

These three areas—aside from networking—can be said to be developing roughly in tandem. That is, advances have been made on all three fronts in such a way that none has crucially delayed the others, although different researchers and developers would say that the key obstacle lies in one or the other of these domains.[29] As the technology has congealed around certain combinations of devices, there has been relatively rapid scientific and technological advance in areas in which the reverse salients of the technology are located ("relatively" in comparison with the range of other devices that have been—or have become—less central to VR development). In other words, there has been a technology push against the several key reverse salients spread across a set of several interrelated areas.

At this stage we can briefly return to our short history of VR because we are now in a position to assess retrospectively why the lull after Sutherland's "ultimate display" came to an end with the first VR systems developed at NASA Ames and VPL: it was at that time that several technologies—small screens with high resolution, increased computer graphics processing power, and more accurate position-tracking—began to be commercially available at relatively low costs. In the same vein, it has more recently become clear that network bandwidth is emerging as a key reverse salient for VR development in the direction of multiuser worlds. In terms of VR systems for single users, however, the main background that has shaped VR development has less to do with social shaping than it does with the cost of the key components on the one hand, and with the focus, over the last decade or so, on visual displays and on human-computer interaction, on the other. Lower costs and improvements in computers and other devices, however, are at most the general preconditions for scientific and technological advance in this field. Put differently, there is nothing "social" about higher computer processing speeds or screens with higher resolutions, and these and other scientific and technological advances have ultimately made VR possible.

Apart from looking back, this is also one of the few points where we may allow ourselves to look ahead and speculate about the future. Display resolution, position-tracking, and computer graphics processing power for generating virtual environments are obstacles that have an endpoint, in the sense that the technology will congeal still further around a particular type of VR system that will set standards both for the technical features of these systems and for the extent to which this technology allows us to manipulate the world. No doubt the process of refinement will continue, but at that point, to paraphrase Weber (1949:112), the light of the great technological problems will move on to other scientific and technological domains.

3

From the Laboratory to Consumer Electronics

How are the institutions engaged in VR research and development shaping the direction of the technology? Before we look in detail at the current scene, it may be useful to recapitulate the brief history presented in the previous chapter in schematic form. Until the mid-to late 1980s, research related to what was to become VR was mainly carried out in a handful of small laboratories nestled inside some of the powerhouses of advanced research in the United States. The main centers included the Massachusetts Institute of Technology, the University of North Carolina at Chapel Hill, Wright-Patterson Air Force Base, and NASA Ames Research Center. Other areas of the information and communication technologies sector have also been dominated by the United States, which has been the primary source for innovation in this sector in the postwar period because of the strength of its economy and cold war competition in advanced technologies.

During the early phase of VR development, from the mid-1980s and into the early 1990s, the picture becomes somewhat more complicated. On the one hand, new research centers in the United States and in Europe (such as the Human Interface Technology Laboratory and the London Parallel Applications Center) and small firms (especially start-ups like VPL and W Industries, which is now called Virtuality) became the driving force behind creating and producing prototype VR systems and components. On the other hand, from about 1992 onward, these smaller institutions have been joined by—or in some cases swallowed up by—the VR efforts of large multinational companies like British Telecom, Matsushita, Sega, and Thompson

CSF, which have been able to dedicate formidable resources toward developing mass market applications of VR (see Figure 3.1).

At present, the horizons of a third phase can be made out.[1] Inexpensive VR systems are being developed for the consumer electronics market, mainly for entertainment. There is also research and development aimed at applications in other areas with large potential markets, such as model-building for engineering design and interactive communications networks. At the same time, a separate and smaller market for more specialized and high-powered VR systems is emerging in areas like medicine (Adam 1993). In these areas of VR research, the shape of VR systems is closely tied to the requirements of the particular area of application. More generally, at this stage, although much effort is still being devoted to building prototypes, research and development have become well-established academic and commercial ventures at dozens of research centers and firms worldwide, with the United States and the U.K. taking the lead in producing the most advanced VR systems.

Laboratory Research

With this background in mind, we can examine the forces shaping VR research in relation to some key examples. Most VR research has either been based in or affiliated with universities. The exceptions are the centers under the aegis of the American military and space programs, and the "garage" or hobbyist efforts of such people as Myron Krueger and Jaron Lanier. To get a sense of some of the strategies the major laboratories have implemented in developing VR, a useful first step is to look at the work of a number of institutions.

Since the take-off of VR technology in the early 1990s, two American research labs have been consistently at the forefront of VR research, the University of North Carolina at Chapel Hill (UNC) and the Human Interface Technology Laboratory (HITLab) at the University of Washington in Seattle. To this we can add, for comparison, two major European research centers, the Fraunhofer Institute in Stuttgart and the London Parallel Applications Center (LPAC). Though the latter are not as prominent worldwide, they have been at the center of European VR efforts.[2]

Apart from NASA Ames, the University of North Carolina and the HITLab are still the most prominent research centers in the United States. The directors of both labs, Thomas Furness and Frederick

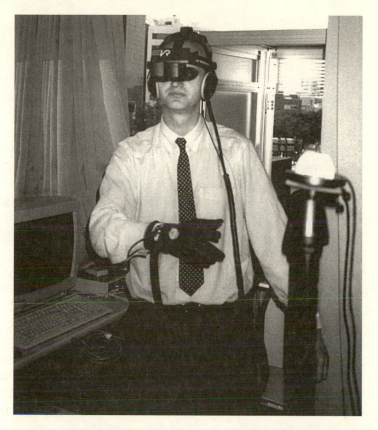

Figure 3.1   The first (nonentertainment) commercial application of VR, the Matsushita kitchen display in Tokyo. This system, which allows customers to select the design of their virtual kitchen, has been in operation since October 1991. (This photograph, taken in September 1994, shows the VPL dataglove and Virtual Research HMD.)

Brooks, were pioneers in developing VR-related technologies during the period before the take-off stage. LPAC and the Fraunhofer Institute were founded much more recently, but both were among the first to establish a European presence on the VR research front. Each of the four has developed particular specialities within VR research: UNC in optical position tracking and computer graphics hardware; the HITLab in retinal displays (displays in which the image is projected directly onto the retina by means of laser technology) and VR software; LPAC in developing parallel computing for VR and investigating "presence" in virtual environments; and the Fraunhofer Institute in using VR for industrial robotics and in manufacturing applications.[3] They are similar in size, and all of them rely on a combination of university and government funding as well as commercial research contracts.[4]

The Fraunhofer Institute in Stuttgart began to explore the use of virtual reality in 1991, starting with the purchase of VPL equipment. In 1993, a VR demonstration center was set up as a project group within the institute.[5] The institute as a whole is mainly devoted to manufacturing technology, and it is one of thirty-three Fraunhofer research institutes in Germany that are supported by the German regional ("Länder") governments. They are nonprofit organizations, ideally self-supporting, and linked with university research departments and industry. Their aim is to undertake research that will bring benefits to German industry and their achievements are highly regarded in Germany.

Promoting industrial applications for VR has proved to be a difficult task for the institute. If there is one phrase that sums up the institute's efforts, it could be the comment made by the director, Hans-Joerg Bullinger, in the closing speech of the first VR conference at the institute in February 1993: "We've got the technology solutions, where are the applications?" By comparison with other Fraunhofer institutes, which are generally acknowledged to be highly successful in translating research into industrial advantage, the institute's VR project has so far registered only limited success at demonstrating uses for VR. In 1993, the institute had announced only one commercial venture, a collaboration to produce a furniture display. It was clear, however, that this was more of a demonstration showpiece rather than a venture with commercial promise.[6] Thus, in spite of considerable outlays and promotional efforts, the VR effort had not yet achieved tangible success in this case.

The strategy of the institute has clearly been to get a head start in developing VR specifically for industry. This is not surprising, given the aims of the Fraunhofer institutes generally and the strength of the Stuttgart institute in the area of robotics in particular. It also makes sense in the light of the concentration of the German economy on manufacturing. Moreover, the use of VR in industry has been widely forecast as one of the most promising areas of application (Kalawsky 1993:330–333; Durlach and Mavor 1995:387–395).

It may be, however, that it is simply too early to transfer VR to industrial users, since unlike with, say, the areas of entertainment or scientific visualization, industry has not had much exposure to VR-like technologies. An obvious exception that immediately springs to mind here is computer-aided design and manufacturing (CAD/CAM). This area, however, is one in which European efforts are far behind those of the United States: the Seattle-based aircraft manufacturer Boeing, for example, used more CAD/CAM tools in the early 1990s than did the whole of European industry put together. One of the HITLab's successful collaborations, for example, has been with Boeing to develop VR systems for use in aircraft design.

Another way of explaining industry's reluctance to use VR might be to refer to the models in economics that try to predict the diffusion of innovations in cases in which strategic advantage can be gained.[7] In industry, the value of VR systems is still an unknown quantity, whereas in the case of entertainment games, for example, it is relatively straightforward to apply a cost/benefit analysis by comparing the cost of games with the income they generate; it therefore may be that industrial applications will not take hold for some time.

Two other German examples can shed further light on the obstacles faced by the Stuttgart institute. The Fraunhofer Institute in Darmstadt, which specializes in computer graphics, also established a VR demonstration center in 1993. It has since been able to attract a variety of users for applications of its systems, such as in interior design, architecture, town planning, and medical training (Astheimer et al. 1994). These are areas that have lent themselves to early experimentation with using VR, and the Darmstadt institute, given its strong background in using computer graphics for scientific visualization, has capitalized on them. The research background of the Stuttgart institute, by contrast, has been in robotics, and its attempts to marry VR systems with robots have depended on the extent to which the link is technically feasible, which is not yet clear.[8]

Another example that can be used for comparison is the Berlin-based group Art+Com. This group, funded partly by the government and partly by industrial sponsorship, has concentrated on producing VR software for architectural and product visualization. In 1992, when VR was still a novelty, Art+Com demonstrated an immersive VR model for the redevelopment of the Potsdamer Platz underground train station in Berlin (making use of a VPL system). The project received considerable publicity and the firm was subsequently commissioned to undertake a number of similar modeling projects. In this case, the high-profile demonstration led to other projects with an "untried" technology. The Fraunhofer institute in Stuttgart, however, has been forced to seek clients in more conservative areas of development.

VR research in Germany has thus been subject to the German model of science-based industry, which tries to "inject" innovation into applied settings. But this model, premised on the value of a science and technology "push," may not be suitable for a technology that has so far shown more of a fit with nonmanufacturing sectors, such as entertainment and scientific visualization. Again, it needs to be added that the problem of finding suitable applications has not been confined to the Fraunhofer Institute in Stuttgart. What the case of the Stuttgart institute illustrates, however, is the difficult position of an institution that is not researching VR systems themselves but is seeking to apply VR to a narrow range of potential applications within industry. However we want to interpret the obstacles to the industrial uses of VR, it is possible that there may be a mismatch between the applications area and the technology here (at least in the technology's current state).

Before we move on to look at other research centers, we should briefly mention some robotics-related VR work in Japan. Susumi Tachi at the Research Center for Advanced Science and Technology (RCAST) at the University of Tokyo has been working on robotics since the 1970s. More recently, Tachi has become interested in using VR for what he calls "real reality,"[9] that is, for helping with real-world tasks such as learning how to operate robots or operating robots from a distance. Like the research at the Stuttgart institute, his work is aimed at industrial users.

Two points apply to RCAST that relate to what has been said about the Stuttgart institute: one is that although Tachi has been undertaking basic research on human factors relating to VR for some years (and even longer in robotics), none of his VR devices have yet been used outside of his lab—although some industries have expressed an interest in his work. The work of the Stuttgart institute, by contrast, at least has been used on a trial basis outside of the lab.

The second point is that Tachi's efforts have been guided and supported by a government-initiated VR feasibility study that includes all the major research centers in Japan interested in or working on VR. The study was initiated by Ministry of Trade and Industry (MITI) and is chaired by Tachi. Nippon Telegram and Telegraph (NTT) and Matsushita are among the participants. Thus, the VR effort in Japan provides support for basic and long-term research that is combined, as we shall see, with a strong interest in the consumer electronics markets for VR. In any case, we have brought up Japanese VR research for industry as an example that shows that a long-term strategy like the Fraunhofer's, which does not seek immediate returns, is not an isolated case.

We can turn now to our second European institution. LPAC was established in 1992, one of a number of centers at the University of London to promote research in applications of parallel computing. This multimillion-pound research program, funded by the government, was aimed at boosting the role of the U.K. in high-performance computing. As with other such programs in the U.K., the government's strategy has been to provide "seed" funding for academic research. The research is expected to become self-financing through links with industry and commerce.

LPAC has been tied to the computer science department at Queen Mary and Westfield College, with the administrative side falling to LPAC and the research carried out by members of the department. One of the main research projects in the department has been concerned with the question of "presence" in virtual environments, which has been investigated partly through research on the importance of having a "virtual body" (Slater and Usoh 1993; Slater, Usoh, and Steed 1994). In addition, there have been two main projects at the center with links to industry: one is a collaboration between LPAC and the Bristol firm Division—a producer of complete VR systems—to devise parallel computing techniques for VR systems.[10] Among other things, Division supplied VR systems in exchange for LPAC's work on evaluating these systems and providing computing expertise.

The second industry-related project has teamed LPAC with the U.K. electronics multinational Thorn-EMI. The aim of this project was to create virtual environments for the architectural design of interior lighting, Thorn-EMI being a major producer of lighting systems. This application demands particularly powerful VR systems since the representation of the effect of several light sources in a virtual environment is a computationally complex task. More specifically, the task requires calculating the impact of each light source on each point in the room, and taking into account the overlapping effect of several light sources and the occlusion of light by objects (Harriss and McKellar 1992). As LPAC's role has been to support a potentially useful area of application (architectural lighting models) and a successful producer of VR systems, its support function and its work on one of the basic issues in VR research ("presence," which will be discussed later in this chapter) have made widely recognized contributions to the advance of VR technology.

In the United States, UNC and the HITLab have both pursued major programs of basic research into various aspects of VR.[11] UNC is located in the region of North Carolina known as the "research triangle," where a number of high-tech industries are clustered. At UNC, the computer science department has been carrying out industry- and government-supported research centered around scientific visualization since the late 1960s. Its sponsors have included the Defence Advanced Research Projects Agency, the National Science Foundation, and firms such as IBM and Intel. In 1967, Frederick Brooks and his colleagues began to develop a display with force-feedback for manipulating computer-generated models of molecular structures (Brooks et al. 1990). This research is ongoing and has become one of the foci of VR-related research. In the late 1980s, the department also began to apply Sutherland's ideas for interactive displays to scientific visualization (Brooks 1988) and it has developed a number of devices in this field.

The VR work at UNC that has recently become most prominent, however, has been the development of powerful hardware and software for high-speed computer graphics. This project, known as Pixel-Flow, has found a commercial outlet through collaboration with the U.K.-based firm Division, which, by incorporating Pixel-Flow into its machines, has produced the most powerful commercially available VR systems to date. The significance of the UNC research was recently underlined in the American National Research Council's report, which pointed out that UNC "is perhaps the only significant university-based computer graphics hardware research group in the United States that is still working" (Durlach and Mavor 1995:290).

The HITLab started in 1989 under the aegis of the Washington Technology Center, an organization set up by the Washington state government on the University of Washington campus to promote links between academic research and industry. As with LPAC, "seed" money in this case was provided to foster a research center that would become self-supporting through links with the private sector. To this end, the HITLab has formed a consortium, the members of which contribute a fixed amount annually ($50,000) in return for collaboration with the lab and privileged access to its research findings. In

1992, for example, there were twelve members, including Boeing, Microsoft, the Port of Seattle, US West Communications (the regional telephone company), and VPL. The number had risen to twenty-seven in 1995. Whereas UNC research has concentrated on medical and scientific visualization applications, some of the main HITLab projects have focused on developing VR tools for airplane design (Boeing), a software platform for VR called VEOS (Virtual Environment Operating System), and the retinal display. The HITLab has also run educational VR projects.

As the HITLab is university-based, its research must become available in the public domain. Thus the VEOS software has been available free of charge, unlike commercial VR software packages, which cost thousands of dollars.[12] The intention behind VEOS was to create a VR software standard that would be useful and enhance the HITLab's prestige. Interestingly, VEOS has not become widely used, partly because the software is written in LISP programming language, a language that is highly regarded among academic researchers in computer science but not very common elsewhere. In fact, it is not clear whether a software standard can emerge in VR as there are so many groups developing VR systems with different specifications and different hardware and software requirements.

The retinal display also deserves comment. The use of laser technology to display an image directly onto the retina potentially offers display technology with a much higher resolution than others in current use. The laser images are of superior quality because laser beams can be controlled in a very precise manner, and scanning them directly onto the retina avoids several problems of conventional displays.

For our purposes, two points are noteworthy: one is that the retinal display involves a long-term commitment to basic research. Although a proof-of-concept monochromatic display has been produced, the technology for a color display, which would be essential for commercial applications, is still many years away. One reason why this technology will take some years to develop is that the required laser technology does not yet exist.[13] The second point is that the idea of displaying images onto the retina or of beaming images directly into people's eyes is widely regarded as a disturbing prospect. In fact, the retinal display is potentially no more harmful to the eye than CRT displays in VR systems or, indeed, those used in conventional television sets (Holmgren and Robinett 1993:183).

All four laboratories are thus to some extent engaged in basic research; that is, in improving the components of VR systems and applications with a view to fundamental and long-term advance. At the same time, the research is also aimed at producing devices that will set standards or become commercially successful and hence eventually yield a significant pay-off in terms of prestige and resources. As we have seen, these research efforts have produced mixed results, and although it is too early to make judgments on this issue, some of the devices and areas of application that have been outlined (Pixel-Flow, scientific visualization) have clearly registered more immediate benefits than others (VEOS, VR for the manufacturing industry).

In examining the development of VR, it is necessary to say something about the relation between university-based research labs and the military establishment. It has already been mentioned that much of the early work on head-up displays for pilots and on flight simulation was undertaken for military purposes. The American military has also played an important role in researching and developing VR applications, especially in relation to battlefield simulation (Sterling 1993; Smith 1994; Stytz 1994) and, more recently, in relation to battlefield surgery by means of telepresence (Satava 1994). The bulk of the military's use of networked simulation and VR, however, has been for training, beginning in the mid-1980s with the DARPA-sponsored SIMNET (SIMulator NETwork) system (Katz 1994) and more recently with the more VR-like (i.e., using head-mounted displays rather than vehicle capsules) Naval Postgraduate School's Networked (NPSNET) VR system (Macedonia et al. 1994).

The American military establishment will no doubt continue to pursue VR development in the areas of training, simulation, hazardous environments, telepresence surgery, and the like and play a key role in these specialized areas. What is perhaps more interesting is that these developments do not overlap on the whole with the non-military dynamic of the technology. It is difficult to envisage how large-scale battlefield simulations might transfer to commercial or civilian settings, aside from contributing to network standards. This separation between military and nonmilitary development applies in other respects too. A number of civilian laboratories have explicitly ruled out working with the military. In the case of the HITLab and LPAC, the decision was made because of staff resistance to collaboration with the military.

At the HITLab, for example, the issue of exploring research related to military work was explicitly raised at a staff meeting, and although the director had extensive experience with military research at Wright-Patterson Air Force Base and did not wish to rule out such collaborative research, HITLab staff unanimously rejected military work (at least for a time—the United States Navy has since become a consortium member at the HITLab for joint development of a training application). Similarly, at an LPAC staff meeting that considered various possibilities for future projects, military projects were explicitly ruled out.

The role of the military in VR is interesting for several reasons. First, it used to be possible to trace advanced research in information and communication technologies to military sources. But as we have seen, in VR the role of the military (apart from its early, pre-takeoff role) has been largely confined to a specific niche, that of high-performance networked VR systems for applications like training simulations. Only a large organization with abundant resources like the military establishment is able to invest large sums to develop the infrastructure for carrying VR over a network (and also develop software standards) without the prospect of short-term returns.[14] The role of the military is thus mainly confined to developing long-term and large-scale systems, and this effort, again, does not currently intersect with the general thrust of civilian VR development.

The second reason military involvement is interesting relates to the clash of cultures between VR and the military. Those who work on VR tend to be much younger than other professionals and, like people in the computer industry as a whole, they often share an "anti-establishment" or nonconformist ethos. As we shall discuss in Chapter 6, it is not difficult to see a link between the colorful and casual attire of computer professionals in VR and the pacific leanings of this group. The rejection of military involvement at a number of university-based research centers is clearly related to this nonconformist ethos.

The resistance to military research at some of the major VR labs is unlikely to prevent military uses of VR. But the antimilitary attitude of researchers may have important consequences for VR, since the early phase of research often plays a decisive role in shaping the direction of technologies. The end of the cold war, too, has brought pressure on research institutes and firms that formerly relied extensively on military contracts to turn their expertise in high technology to advantage in civilian markets.

Apart from the examples already given, a number of companies that used to develop simulators for military purposes, such as Hughes

Rediffusion and Evans & Sutherland, are now also working on entertainment applications using simulators and VR. With the exception of training simulations and the development of remote battlefield surgery, the role of the military is therefore limited, and the dynamic of military research and development in VR has become as contradictory as the role of the military in post-cold war society generally: caught between seeking new roles like surveillance, on the one hand, and demonstrating civilian benefits, on the other.[15]

The Dynamic of VR R&D

At this point, we can put the research efforts of the labs already mentioned into the wider context of VR R&D. A first step is to outline the positions of the United States, Japan, and the European Community. The United States currently has the strongest program of VR research and the strongest computer industry as a whole. Its research and commercial efforts in VR, however, are geared toward short-term profit, unlike those in Japan and the European Community. And although American firms produce many important components for VR systems, such as head-mounted displays, position-trackers, VR software packages, and computer graphics workstations, two U.K. companies (Division and Virtuality) are among the main producers of commercially available VR systems.

Division and Virtuality, plus the U.K. firm Superscape, which produces VR software, are also the only VR firms listed on the stock exchange. Thus the U.K. currently has a strong position in marketable VR systems, whereas its research base, at least in terms of resources, is comparatively weak. An important source of funding for basic VR research in the United Kingdom, interestingly, is the European Community rather than the British government. So, for example, the VIR-TUOSI project for networked VR has been partly funded by E.C. initiatives.

Germany and Japan, by contrast, are devoting abundant resources toward long-term and industrially oriented VR projects.[16] So far, their efforts have lagged in developing workable prototypes or marketable systems and products. Other countries in the European community, apart from the U.K., are playing a secondary role in VR R&D, and the very advanced research in Japan will take some time to translate into VR systems and applications. The exception, for Japan, is VR entertainment games, often developed in collaboration with

U.S. and U.K. partners. It is conceivable that the market in VR games, so far dominated by the U.K.'s Virtuality, may become radically transformed by the introduction of home VR games and may be captured by Sega and Nintendo.

A different picture emerges if we look at the overall thrust of technological and commercial development. Although the main push for innovation has come from the research centers, the most important market for VR has been entertainment games, which are technically not very advanced or sophisticated. According to one estimate, VR for entertainment uses accounts for $190.3 million of a total market for VR of $257 million in 1995.[17] At the same time, it is unlikely that technical standards for VR systems will emerge (with the possible exception of those required for health and safety reasons) that might establish the system developed by a particular research center or firm as an unchallengeable technical or market leader. There are simply too many approaches to VR in competition with one another. Hence, too, the question of which kinds of systems or devices may become dominant or direction-giving remains open.

The main impetus for VR development, therefore, remains dependent both on technological advance and on the market for VR systems. The two broad trends that can be discerned are toward low-cost and unsophisticated VR systems for the consumer market and more technically complex and expensive systems for specialized markets. Other major factors that play a large role in VR development are the potential appeal of home entertainment VR games and the emergence of networked VR systems. The first is possibly influenced by health and safety issues and moral panics regarding these games (which will be discussed in Chapter 4) and the second by the possible convergence of technologies such as interactive television and computer mediated communication. But this takes us beyond the VR R&D landscape that is currently shaping the direction of the technology.

As we move on to examine the contexts in which VR is used, it may be useful to bear several features of VR research and development in mind. The first is that although research on VR has been mainly carried out in academic settings, it has been heavily geared toward—or undertaken in collaboration with—the private sector. This has not always been the case in the information and communication technology sector (it may suffice to remind ourselves here of the example of the influence of the military on high-speed computing). Governments have also taken an active interest in promoting VR, stirred by the fear that they may be left behind in this important area.[18]

Yet the various national programs or recommendations for action have not had a decisive impact on VR: The two broad trends just identified, for example, have had little to do with government initiatives. Likewise, as we have seen, the military contribution to VR development has only been significant in limited areas, such as training and networked VR, during the take-off phase, and it has not overlapped more recently with civilian VR. The pattern of VR research and development is thus likely to continue to be shaped by the several forces that have been described here, including commercial pressures on the "low" end of the VR market, the competition among a number of research laboratories, and the technology "pushes" for specialist applications and systems.

The Body in the Virtual World

At this point it may be useful to give a concrete illustration of how research is shaping VR systems. One issue that is still open-ended in VR is the representation of the user in the virtual world. When virtual reality first became publicly known in the early 1990s, the pictures of the technology that appeared in newspaper articles typically showed VR systems as consisting of a head-mounted display, a bodysuit, and a glove. The image that was often used was of the VR system developed by Jaron Lanier, featuring a bodysuit and glove with sensors, whereby the user's whole body was represented inside the virtual world. More recently, however, the image of VR systems has changed. It has come to be replaced with a VR system consisting of a head-mounted display and a hand-held 3–D mouse. The bodysuit and glove no longer seem to be essential features of VR systems.

This change in image does not necessarily mean that VR systems no longer include representations of the user's body, since, as we shall see, users often have bodies in the virtual world without wearing a bodysuit and glove. But whether the body should be represented at all, and if so, in what form, is still an open question among researchers and developers of VR systems. What is certain is that although the variety of VR systems has mushroomed since the early 1990s, the bodysuit, and to a lesser extent the glove, has fallen into almost complete neglect. Among the hundreds of laboratories and firms now producing VR systems and components, less than a handful are developing or manufacturing bodysuits. Likewise, gloves seem to be confined to specialized VR applications, whereas the vast majority of commercial VR systems employ hand-held 3-D mice. This is surprising, not least because the bodysuit has continued to generate media interest in VR, particularly in connection with "virtual sex." As we shall see, the range of options for representing the body has important consequences for the direction of VR development and thus for the social implications of this technology.

We can take our first example from the realm of academic research. The person who has done most to investigate the question of the importance of the body in virtual worlds is Mel Slater of Queen Mary and Westfield College in London, although the body is only one part of a wider investigation into "presence" in VR. Slater and his colleagues in the computer science department have published a number of essays on "presence" and the body that are based on trials in which subjects were asked to report on their experience of presence in a virtual world (Slater and Usoh 1993; Slater, Usoh, and Steed 1994).

Without going into this research in any detail, Slater argues that having a representation of the body in the virtual world is an important requirement of VR systems. It needs to be added immediately that what Slater means by a body is a three-dimensional computer-generated image of *a* body, rather than one generated by means of the input from sensors on a bodysuit and glove. This type of body in the virtual world is shown in Figures 3.2 and 3.3. These two photographs are from one of the trials carried out by Slater, Usoh, and Steed (see 1994:130–144) to investigate presence by means of the concept of "stacking environments." In this trial, subjects are asked to don a virtual HMD within the virtual environment in order to enter a "deeper" environment. This process can be repeated several times and then the question can be posed: "To what extent is their sense of presence correlated with the depth of environment visited?"(1994:1).

The VR system that Slater has used in his trials consists of a head-mounted display and a hand-held 3-D mouse. The software used with this system generates the image of a body that moves in accordance with the user's head and hand positions. The user moves the body forward in the virtual world by pushing the button on the 3-D mouse. In Slater's trials, one group of users was represented in the virtual world with an arrow cursor—which is a common method of representing users in VR systems—whereas the other group had a full

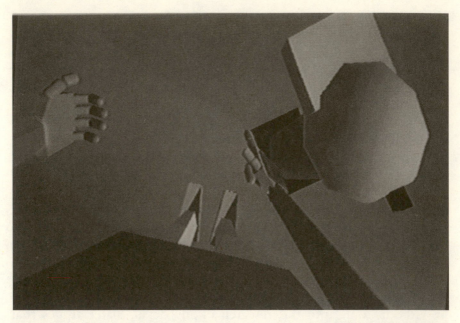

Figure 3.2   *Looking down at the virtual body and the virtual HMD, which is on a pedestal. Courtesy of the computer science department at Queen Mary and Westfield College*

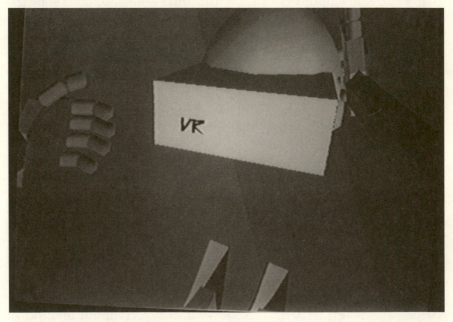

Figure 3.3   *Picking up the virtual HMD with a virtual arm. Courtest of the computer science department of Queen Mary and Westfield College.*

virtual body. Both groups were asked to perform a number of tasks, including "walking a plank over a virtual precipice"(Slater and Usoh 1993:226). The subjects' performance was evaluated during the trial by observers and by means of questionnaires that users filled out afterwards.

Again, without going into the details of this research, what the results indicate according to Slater (albeit in a preliminary form) is that having a virtual body enhances the user's sense of presence. Slater, like other VR researchers, argues that the sense of presence of the user is influenced both by external and internal factors. That is, the VR machine must of course provide a realistic sense of being in a virtual world (Slater and Usoh 1993:222; see also Barfield et al. 1995). This requires high-resolution displays, accurate position-tracking devices that avoid "lag" between the user's movements and the response of the virtual world, realistic-looking computer-generated environments, and the like. There are also internal factors, such as the expectations which users may bring to VR systems before they use them (Slater and Usoh 1993:231 and passim). But in addition, Slater's research shows that apart from these factors, having a virtual body provides a greater sense of presence than not having one.

However this question of the measurement of presence in the virtual world may come to be resolved, the point is that Slater's ideas and trials relate to one specific form of the technology, in this case an HMD and hand-held 3-D mouse. This type of VR system only allows a certain kind of representation of the user's body. In Slater's system, the input from the user's body consists of the position of the user's head and hand, plus the image of *a* body. This is different both from a system such as Lanier's, which uses a bodysuit to represent the movements of the user's actual body, as well as from systems in which the user is represented only by an arrow cursor, for example, or by the shape of a stationary body shown sitting. The representations of virtual bodies in VR systems affects how users interact with the virtual world—and what they can *do* in that world.

In connection with Slater's research, one concrete illustration of this point is a virtual table tennis game designed by one of the research students in his department. Using a hand-held 3-D mouse as a racket, a user can play against a computer-generated opponent. The computer-generated opponent, in the shape of a racket, is programmed to return the ball.

What is interesting is that having a virtual body has specific benefits in this case, since players not only get a "natural" sense of play from having a virtual arm and racket but are also able to locate their virtual bodies in relation to the virtual table. That it is better to play with a virtual body rather than without one may have to do with the fact that table tennis players are used to playing with a body in the real world, or it may be that the player benefits from having a sense of spatial orientation in the virtual world. The usefulness of having a body in the virtual table tennis game, however, is beyond doubt to those who are familiar with using various types of VR systems and who experience this environment both with and without a body.

It is worth mentioning that one of the reasons Slater has pursued this line of research has to do with the circumstances in which he first encountered VR technology. When he used the initial VR system that was delivered to his department, what immediately struck him about the experience was that he did not have a virtual body. To remedy this, he opted for using a computer-generated body in connection with the system. Yet his preferred solution does not explain why he used a 3-D mouse rather than a dataglove, for example, to represent a virtual hand. When I asked Slater why he had opted for the 3-D mouse, he told me that he had considered using a dataglove, but that in practice, gloves tended to malfunction. Moreover, he thought that users tended to perceive gloves as an encumbrance rather than as a "natural" interface.[19] Hence his research has concentrated almost exclusively on the combination of HMD, hand-held 3-D mouse, and computer-generated body.

A second example of how the body is represented in the virtual world can be taken from the realm of VR games. Games have so far been the most common application of VR technology. The way the user's body has been represented has taken various forms in VR games, from a full three-dimensional computer-generated body to an arrow cursor. In some games, like Evans & Sutherland's hang glider, the user "flies" through the virtual world without a virtual body. Other games, like Straylight's Cybertron, use an eye-level perspective. Another option gives the user the impression of being airborne and viewing the virtual world from above, as in Sega's VR-1 Space Mission. Games can also be differentiated by whether players play standing up or sitting down. Some stand-up games, like Virtuality's Dactyl Nightmare, allow players to walk around in the virtual world by pushing the button of a hand-held joystick. In this case, the game features a three-dimensional computer-generated body. In sit-down games, such as Sega's VR-1 Space Mission and Virtuality's Flying Aces, users sit in a mock-up space-vehicle or airplane cockpit, and although they can see their computer-generated virtual bodies, those bodies remain stationary whereas the vehicles move through the virtual world by means of joystick control (see Figure 3.4).[20]

Unlike some VR systems that are designed to relate to practical tasks in the real world, VR games represent fantasy worlds. Moreover, from a technical point of view, they are far less sophisticated than VR systems used in research such as Slater's. Even so, the various ways in which the user's body is represented in these systems provide different experiences of virtual worlds: for example, in games in which the user sits in a virtual vehicle, the user's (real) body has the sensation of being in a vehicle, as in a simulator game. The difference between the experience of sitting in a "moving" vehicle and "flying" or "walking" by means of a hand-held joystick is self-evident. Thus, the degrees of control or interaction that are possible in the virtual world depend on which bodily representations and modes of navigation are used.

Multiplayer VR games provide another way of highlighting the difference that the representations of bodies can make in the experience of virtual worlds. Games like Virtuality's Legend Quest, for example, allow up to four players to share the same virtual world and feature

Figure 3.4   VR-1 Space Mission at Sega's Joypolis arcade, Yokohama.

computer-generated virtual bodies controlled by means of a joystick. Interestingly, one of the difficulties in these games is that players need to get used to carrying out tasks (such as destroying monsters) in close proximity to one another. This can often be awkward since virtual bodies can "get in each other's way," which produces a disorientating effect for players. Shared virtual worlds, in which the visual representations of users overlap, therefore demonstrate that having a virtual body can have disadvantages as well as advantages.

It is not only the shape of virtual bodies that matters in the experience of virtual worlds, but also the level of detail with which they are represented. Some VR games represent other players or the virtual opponents in a cartoonlike way. That is, the figures in some games appear box-like and the main parts of the body are surfaces shaded in a single color (for example, in Legend Quest—see Figure 5.1). Other games, however, represent virtual opponents in much more detail, achieving an effect of photo-realism by means of computer graphics techniques like texturing and shading (Virtuality's Zone Hunter). At the other extreme, some VR systems (in this case from the applications area of cooperative work rather than gaming) such as the Distributed Interactive Virtual Environment (DIVE) being developed by Fahlen and his colleagues, represent users as rectangular blocks with cartoon-like eyes and a smile, nicknamed "Blockies" (1994:69).

Another variant, which has recently been introduced, is a facility for importing a two-dimensional photograph of a real person's face and attaching it to the virtual body in the virtual world (Fahlen 1994:69). In short, virtual bodies can have the appearance of anything from a block shape to a detailed photo-realistically rendered or photographic image. How users react to these different representations of bodies varies considerably: if we use the example of shared virtual environments again, coordinating one's activities with a block-like figure, for instance, is different from coordinating one's activities with a photo-realistically rendered figure.

A number of reasons can be given for why the body is represented in these different ways in VR games. One is that it is "expensive" in terms of computer processing power to generate a moving virtual body, which is of obvious importance in a competitive market like entertainment games. Researchers like Slater, by contrast, may have access to high-powered machines and plentiful computer programming resources, so that generating a virtual body is more a question of trade-offs against the other computer processing requirements of the VR system.[21]

Another factor relates to navigation. In the case of games, it is possible to say that allowing the user to "walk" around in the virtual world makes for an exploratory style of play, as opposed to the more engrossing experience of "flying" (these differences will be discussed more fully in Chapter 5). This is important in virtual reality games, which typically last only for a few minutes. Since VR games are competing with other highly engrossing forms of entertainment, such as simulators and screen-based computer games, they have tended to follow the same format as other games by featuring space vehicles, flight simulations, shoot-'em-ups, and the like. In other words, VR games have avoided more exploratory modes of play. For both technical and commercial reasons then, the representation of the virtual body in VR games has been shaped by the demand for an engrossing experience.

A third example that sheds interesting light on the issues around the virtual body is Susumu Tachi's telepresence research project (Tachi and Yasuda 1994; Watson 1994:4). Tachi has developed a telepresence system in which the user, who sits in what looks like a dentist's chair, wearing an HMD and holding a hand-controller, operates a robot that is approximately twenty feet away.[22] The robot consists of a mechanical arm and two video cameras mounted on a stationary homomorphic stand. Thus the user's view and the movement of the user's arm are translated into the movement of the robot's head and arm.

Tachi's telepresence system has two particularly interesting features: The first feature allows users to maintain their own perspective on the action—that is, users can watch the robot perform—or they can adopt the robot's perspective. Seeing from the robot's point of view gives a participant the extremely uncanny sensation of being able to see his or her own body, some distance away, sitting in a chair while moving the head and arms. The second is that the image inside the head-mounted display can be either a (real) video image or a (computer-generated) virtual one. Thus, in one demonstration of the system, the user is asked to stack wooden blocks using the robot arm, and this action can be switched back and forth between a video image of the blocks or a computer-generated image.

One of Tachi's main concerns has been to investigate how effectively users can operate the robot by carrying out various experiments to measure task performance. What is important, for our purposes, is that Tachi's system presents yet another way of thinking about the user's body in the virtual world that differs from those discussed so far. Tachi's aim is to produce a system that allows the user to carry out tasks in a virtual environment that are closely related to tasks in the real world—for example, manufacturing tasks.

For users to accomplish these tasks, it is essential that Tachi's VR system produce a virtual world that can be manipulated effectively. What matters for these tasks, however, is not the representation of the user's whole virtual body. Although users see representations of their bodies while sitting in the chair, what is important in this virtual world is mastering hand-eye coordination—being able to grasp objects and manipulate them by means of precise position tracking of the head and hand. Thus, the user is able to gain familiarity with carrying out difficult tasks in the virtual world—such as stacking blocks or, another typical robot task, rearranging eggs (Watson 1994:4)—and to be able to do them fairly quickly.

For Tachi then, there is an emphasis on providing a virtual body that consists of an effective head and arm, the arm in this case being a hand-gripper with force-feedback. This visual representation of the body differs both from Slater's, which does not have force-feedback, and from the various options that represent the body in VR games. It is interesting to note, incidentally, that Tachi refers to VR games as "fantasy reality" and describes his research, by contrast, as aiming at "real reality."[23]

What he means is that it is easy to give the user the illusion of being in a fantastical virtual world, but to convey a realistic virtual world in which the user carries out practical tasks requires a far more sophisticated VR system. For instance, this applies to cases in which VR technology is used to train people by having them practice tasks—such as performing surgical operations—first in the virtual world, so that they can then be more skilled when it comes to performing them in the real world. Such realistic virtual worlds will make considerable demands on virtual world design.[24]

Tachi's VR system is undoubtedly more complex than those used in VR games, but again, what is important for our purposes is that in this VR system, the body is represented in yet another way. Although the representation is similar to that of other systems in that it features a computer-generated body, the emphasis of the virtual body is on the link between visual tasks and manual gripping tasks. It is perhaps futile to speculate whether ultimately, in an industrial application of VR involving a slaved robot, a full representation of the user's body will be useful or not.

Whatever form the representation of the user takes, it is bound to have an impact on the user's experience. And although neither Tachi's nor Slater's VR systems are in everyday use yet, they, along with the systems used for entertainment, point to a variety of VR experiences: In Tachi's system, hand-eye coordination is all-important, whereas Slater's system is designed to enhance the user's subjective feeling of presence. In contrast, in the experiences provided by VR games, the feeling of presence relates closely to the technical sophistication of the games and to their content. Perhaps users are also influenced by expectations that they bring from other games like simulator rides and computer games.

Different representations of the body in VR systems can thus be found in different contexts in which VR is used. Slater is trying to find out under what conditions users experience presence in the virtual world. Tachi's system aims to improve the performance of practical tasks in real-world situations. VR games systems create the impression that the user is experiencing high speeds, shooting opponents, and the like. These different contexts require different methods of representing the user's body, different machine characteristics, and different types of virtual worlds. These characteristics, in turn, have important consequences for VR system users that relate to both technical factors, such as computational demands or tracking accuracy, and to psychological or social factors—perhaps, above all, users' familiarity with other, similar technologies and its effect on their experience of VR systems.

As we have now presented a range of implications of various representations of the user's body in different VR systems, it remains to spell out the wider context in which the impact of these representations makes itself felt. The limited amount of control that users typically exercise in VR games is similar to that in existing computer-based games. But VR systems are also different from other computer games, inasmuch as they cut players off from their surroundings. The sense of bodily presence in the world of the VR game, therefore, extends the capacity of existing machines to transport players into a world of computer-generated leisure, even if only for short periods.

VR systems used in research projects, in turn, differ from VR games: The VR system used in Slater's research, for example, represents a considerable advance over Sutherland's in allowing investigations into the nature of the experience of computer-generated environments.[25] Tachi's system, finally, advances this understanding in relation to practical tasks in simulated worlds. The insights gained from these two types of systems have mainly been applied in prototype VR machines, whereas VR games have migrated into entertainment arcades by the hundreds. And again, VR games are currently poised to invade (or to be invited into) the living room, in the form of home entertainment systems that are currently being produced by several manufacturers.

All three types of VR systems are similar inasmuch as they immerse users in virtual worlds, cutting their senses off from the real world and enabling them to interact with a virtual one. Yet, as we have seen, this similarity hides major differences, particularly in the degree of control users have over the virtual world and how the sense of presence and interaction affects this control.

No single factor accounts for the diversity of virtual bodies. The representation of the user's body, like other areas of VR, is subject to the interlocking of refining and manipulating, or to the "fit" between the development of VR devices and what they enable users to do in the virtual world (or how they constrain them). Both technological as well as social factors will continue to determine the types of artifacts and the types of virtual bodies that are developed. Yet from what has been said, it is clear that certain options are becoming more prevalent. To underline this point, it can be recalled that the technological option this section began with, the bodysuit, seemed predestined to guide the future of VR development. The bodysuit, however, is no longer among the main technological options being pursued. More recently, other means of representing the body, with all that they imply for users, have been developing in a few dominant directions. How these trends unfold in the future does not depend on research and gaming contexts alone. They also depend on the extent to which VR systems become diffused throughout—or again, the extent to which they migrate into—the worlds of entertainment, industry, and other areas.[26]

4

Virtual Worlds and Everyday Realities: Education and Games

Learning with VR

Give the tools to the young: before they are conditioned; before they are seduced and bemused. (Clark 1992:9)

Up until now, VR has only been used in a limited number of settings, aside from that of entertainment games. If training were to be included under the rubric of education, that would make education the second-largest area of VR application after entertainment. The use of VR in battlefield simulation and vehicle simulation, for example, probably accounts for more everyday VR applications than any other area, apart from games. In this chapter, however, we shall define education in the more narrow sense, referring to schools, where so far there have been only a handful of pilot projects. These, however, have generated an enormous amount of interest, both from the media and from educators. We will focus on three education projects, the West Denton High School in Newcastle, the Shepherd School in Nottingham, and the Human Interface Technology Laboratory's summer school in Seattle.

Before each project is described in detail, some general comments are called for. Here as elsewhere, our main concern will be with the relationship between VR technology and the social context. It is still too early to attempt an evaluation of the effectiveness of VR as a teaching tool.[1] Instead, the focus will be on how VR systems are coming to be used in these settings: How do they fit into existing teaching practices? How are pupils and staff responding to them? What patterns of VR use are emerging? And finally, how do these systems compare with other uses of VR? One issue to bear in mind throughout is that unlike the use of VR in entertainment, where virtual worlds are, so to speak, prefabricated, in education (at least in the case of the Seattle and West Denton projects), pupils were able to build their own worlds. Questions about VR in education thus provide a good opportunity to find out what possibilities there are for creating different kinds of virtual worlds, a topic that will be pursued further in the following chapter.

The first project to use VR in a classroom took place at the Human Interface Technology Laboratory (HITLab) at the University of Washington in Seattle in 1991. We have already introduced the HIT-Lab as one of the key institutions in VR research. The idea of teaching with VR, in this case, was intended as "a first step in evaluating the potential of VR as a learning environment" (Bricken and Byrne 1992:1). The format of the summer school consisted of week-long sessions during which pupils would spend four days building their virtual worlds on desktop computers and on the final day they would experience their worlds on the lab's immersive VR system. The summer school and other educational VR projects have been ongoing ever since, and the HITLab has now established a VR learning center.[2]

The resources for the summer school project, apart from the HIT-Lab and pupils' fees, have come partly from public institutions (the Pacific Science Center) and partly from the private sector (the US West telephone company, a HITLab consortium member). The 1992 sessions, for example, consisted of approximately twenty-five pupils between 10 and 15 years of age who were mainly drawn from the Seattle area, plus about a dozen staff members.

The daily timetable was organized around activities such as computer graphics, electronic music, and VR itself. The end goal, however, was to build a virtual world. Pupils worked in small groups on the process of world-building and were encouraged to work as teams. The equipment for building worlds was Swivel 3-D software (see Kalawsky 1993:211–212), and the immersive system consisted of a VPL system with a glove or hand-held 3-D mouse (see Figure 4.1).[3]

Several features of this project deserve to be highlighted. One is that the process of learning how to build virtual worlds was achieved in a relatively short time. Pupils put together their worlds in less than a week. They were given an "allowance" of polygons and within this limit could build any world they liked. A sense of the kinds of worlds pupils built can be gleaned from the names they chose, such as Moon Colony, Mid-evil [i.e., medieval] Spacestation, and Neighborhood. When I had an opportunity to fly through some of these worlds in the

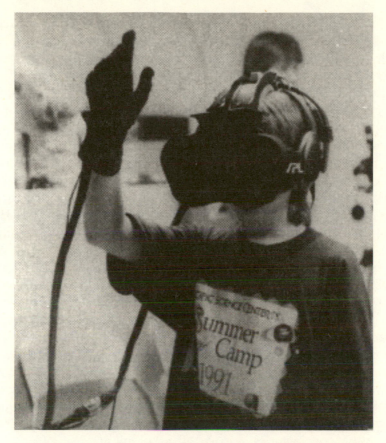

Figure 4.1   A pupil from the Pacific Science Center/HITLab summer school using a VPL HMD and dataglove. (This photograph was taken in 1991. Courtesy of the Human Interface Technology Laboratory.)

lab, they appeared imaginative and contained many outlandish features.

Before we focus on some other features of the HITLab project, let us look briefly at the project at the West Denton High School, a public sector secondary school located on a large housing estate on the outskirts of Newcastle-upon-Tyne. The school accommodates 650 students aged 13 to 19. West Denton places particular emphasis on information technology and is well equipped with video-making facilities, computer-aided design (CAD) software, personal computers, and other information technology equipment. The school otherwise is not well endowed with resources and is attended by pupils whose performance has been below average during their primary education.

It is nevertheless a school that prides itself on innovative teaching methods, and it has a very good record of achievement among Newcastle schools (City of Newcastle-upon-Tyne Education Department 1991:11 and appendices 1–3).

The main driving force behind the virtual reality project at West Denton was its headmaster, Michael Clark. His enthusiasm about changing existing methods of teaching (which he calls "boring") has provided much of the impetus behind the school's focus on information technology. It is easy to get the impression that the VR project, like others at the school, was created to a large extent thanks to Clark's personal charisma. This is borne out by the fact that the VR project, which was a flagship project of the school in 1991–1992, came to a standstill after Clark left the school to take a more challenging headmastership in London in September 1992.

When Clark first heard of VR in 1991, he began to contact the manufacturers of VR equipment and to seek funds from industry and from public institutions. Once the resources were in place—he obtained £47,500 (approximately $75,000) from a government training program and a matching sum from a local engineering firm and the regional development council—he acquired equipment and software. Clark obtained two desktop VR systems: the Virtus Walkthrough software to run on an Apple Macintosh computer and the Dimension Superscape Toolkit (the firm Dimension has since become Superscape), which runs on a customized personal computer supplied by Dimension and includes a spaceball as an input device (see Figure 4.2).[4]

Both suppliers, especially Dimension, supported the project with staff and expertise, and have, in turn, been rewarded with considerable publicity from the project.

It needs to be emphasized that both VR systems in this case were of the desktop type, using a desktop personal computer with a mouse or a spaceball input device. But as we have pointed out, it is still not clear what final shape VR will take and thus how important these distinctions are. It is also worth mentioning that some manufacturers of immersive systems have ensured that the software for their systems can be used in conjunction with desktop computer displays. Conversely, the software produced by some manufacturers of desktop systems can be used in conjunction with immersive systems. So, for example, the virtual environments created on Superscape software can be transferred (or "ported") to immersive VR systems. Superscape

Figure 4.2   Pupils at the West Denton High School using the Virtus and Dimension desktop VR systems while the headmaster, Michael Clark, looks on (photograph taken in 1992).

systems are now also available for use with an inexpensive HMD (although this combination was not available in 1992). And again, there is a range of devices and software packages that fall "in between" the immersive and desktop categories. We shall return to the issue of the different systems later. In the meantime, let us consider the label VR in this case as unproblematic.

Pupils attending West Denton are drawn from the immediate area and they pursue the standard subjects for the National Curriculum in Britain, which culminate in taking Advanced ("A") level examinations for the General Certificate of Secondary Education (GCSE) and other vocational qualifications. The subjects are of the pupils' choosing, but at West Denton, the emphasis tends to be on vocational subjects such as computer science and art and design. West Denton also has a number of pupils pursuing postsecondary diploma courses (Business and Technical Education Council Certificate or BTEC) in art and design. These pupils made up a large proportion of those using the VR systems.

Teaching with VR began in March 1992 and several projects have continued ever since.[5] Three staff members were assigned to work with the VR project on a regular basis, and several other staff members were involved indirectly. Students tended to work in small groups with the two systems and less often on their own. They worked for several hours per week on the design of virtual worlds.

VR was intended for use in several areas of the curriculum—language, for which a French virtual city was developed, and art and design, for which students created a virtual sculpture gallery. Yet the main project to reach completion in the summer of 1992 was the Dangerous Workplace world, a factory with moving machinery and forklifts.[6] This world was built in collaboration with NEI Parsons, the sponsoring engineering firm, and was created particularly with a view to learning about safety at work. The collaboration involved pupils visiting the firm's factory to get a sense of the relation between the virtual world and the model on which it was based. NEI Parsons employees, in turn, were able to visit the school and work to help design the "factory."

The VR project was confined to one classroom within the school, with both systems set side by side on a long worktable in a large, windowless room (unlike with other VR settings, the lack of windows mainly had to do with preventing theft of the computer equipment). In practice, staff were almost always present when students were working on VR. Lessons were of variable duration, although students would typically spend between fifteen minutes and an hour using the systems. Both in content and in its place in the curriculum, VR was part of a normal course of study throughout the school year rather than a separate skill or subject. In the school year ending in the summer of 1992, approximately 35 students participated in the project.

At this point, we can begin to make some comparisons between West Denton and the HITLab. One difference between this and the Seattle summer school was that in West Denton, the virtual worlds were all representations of real world phenomena, although this was a product of the aims of the curriculum rather than because of pupils' choice. In contrast, the Seattle pupils mainly built fantasy worlds. One of the similarities between the two programs was that pupils learned to design worlds on the systems within a matter of hours. In fact, teachers in both programs were not always of much help, as they knew little more than their pupils did about world design. Pupils' autonomy and their immediate sense of achievement in learning quickly to design worlds, seems to account for a large part of their enthusiasm for VR, especially compared with other school work.

To carry these comparisons further, we can bring in the results of questionnaires that were undertaken at West Denton and compare them with responses to a questionnaire completed at the HITLab summer school.[7] When an equal number of West Denton pupils, some of whom had and some of whom had not used the VR system, were asked what kind of virtual worlds they would like to build, their answers fell into three main categories of roughly equal size: historical worlds, contemporary worlds with utopian features, and futuristic worlds (some terrestrial and some in space).[8] What is noticeable here is that pupils who had worked only on quite "practical" worlds were keen to use VR in this way. This may give some indication of the kinds of things young people may wish to do with VR, whether they have used VR or not.

Several other differences between the two schools can be highlighted. The Seattle summer school, for example, took place outside of the normal school setting, and the pupils who chose to attend did so because of their interest in computing. However, for pupils at West Denton High School, computing was part of the curriculum. Thus most of the West Denton pupils spent between one and three hours per week during the school term using computers.

Pupils at both schools said that they wanted to use VR again and that they preferred using VR over playing computer games, using (non-VR) computer programs, and watching television. And again, at both schools, pupils said that they would prefer building virtual worlds to using worlds already built. Finally, only a very small proportion commented on the poverty of the display or on disorientation or dizziness in using VR, despite the fact that these problems are high on the agenda of VR researchers and developers. It may also be noted that West Denton pupils did not, on the whole, comment on the lack of a head-mounted display. In other words, the idea that desktop VR should not be seen as VR did not occur to them.

Another important difference between the two school settings is that the Seattle school allowed pupils to build virtual worlds from start to finish. At West Denton, by contrast, pupils worked on parts of the virtual worlds for the duration of the lesson and other pupils and staff would continue to build them later. It was therefore difficult for students to get a sense of building an entire virtual world. Pupils in the two programs received quite different impressions of VR technology from these two ways of integrating VR into the learning process, but this is a point that we shall come back to later.

An observation made by Chris Byrne, one of the principal staff members of the Seattle school, is useful: she pointed out that on one occasion when she allowed some of the pupils to experience an immersive world during the middle of the week (rather than at the end), they got back to the job of building virtual worlds with much more enthusiasm. That is, knowing about immersive VR systems and VR experiences makes a difference as to how pupils regard their world-building task. It is therefore important to consider how VR technology is best integrated within a program of learning and exploring, or, more specifically, how this integration can sustain pupils' motivation to use the technology.

One effect of using VR in the classroom in both cases was that because teachers were no more skilled in world-building than pupils, the technology promoted student-centered learning. The learning style may also relate to the educational philosophies of those implementing the programs. Michael Clark's attitude can be gleaned from the following remarks about the use of information technology in education:

> That is where the future lies . . . in the presentation and manipulation of information in as yet unknown ways. . . . Give the tools to the young: before they are conditioned; before they are seduced and bemused. Technology is too important for technologists just as education is too important to leave to educationalists. (1992:9)

Similarly, Chris Byrne spoke of "empowering" pupils through the use of this technology (see also Bricken 1991).

"Empowering" pupils has also been part of the pilot project with virtual reality in special needs education at the Shepherd School, but this project has also had a more specific aim.[9] The Shepherd School is the largest special needs school in Britain, with over two hundred pupils with severe and profound learning difficulties. They vary widely in terms of ability, and the age of pupils who used VR ranged from five to nineteen. The VR system at the Shepherd School, as at West Denton, was of the desktop type, using Dimension software in conjunction with mouse and spaceball input devices. The Dimension software was modified for educational use by the Virtual Reality Applications Research Team (VIRART) at Nottingham University, which was responsible for the technical side of the project.[10]

The Shepherd School employs the Makaton system of alternative communication, authored by Margaret Walker (1987), which is the standard system used in British special needs schools. The system uses hand signs and iconic symbols that stand for objects to teach language and communication concepts. It aims to develop communication skills among people with very different abilities and can be used in connection with a variety of learning disabilities, such as autism, mental retardation, specific language disorder, acquired neurological problems, and multiple sensory handicap.

The system consists of vocabulary and is designed to be taught through a series of stages with increasing complexity. Thus it tries to develop not only language skills but also more sophisticated general communication skills. At the Shepherd School, as at West Denton, the VR system is integrated with existing teaching methods and with the existing curriculum. The virtual worlds in this case consist of roomlike spaces in which different objects—such as a mug, a ball, and a television set—are displayed. The Makaton symbol for the object is displayed in another part of the room. If pupils succeed in matching the Makaton symbol with the object by navigating through the room, the thumbs up sign appears (see Figures 4.3, 4.4).

In the case of VR use at the Shepherd School, it is important to touch briefly on the theories that underlie the processes of human learning. In recent years, cognitive psychology has emerged as the most prominent approach within this field. Moreover, with respect to language acquisition, the Piagetian perspective, which stresses the interaction between the individual and the external environment, has proved particularly useful (Jones 1995:250–252). It is also worth mentioning the relevance of debates about language, which revolve around the question of how pictures may best be used to acquire language skills. Without going into these theories or debates,[11] the point to note for our purposes is that Shepherd School pupils were able to exercise a sense of control in the virtual environment, since they could interact with the objects and icons on the computer screen.

It has been noted in other learning contexts that interaction with computers using graphics and animation enhances pupils' sense of control (Garland 1982). Furthermore, because the representation of objects in a virtual environment is more "realistic" than in a conventional picture, active participation also helps to overcome the limitations of other learning methods. This interaction and realism were made possible because of the way in which the Makaton system of

Figure 4.3   A Shepherd School pupil navigating by means of a joystick.

hand signs and symbols could be translated into a three-dimensional
virtual environment that could be manipulated.

It needs to be emphasized that the Shepherd School project, like
the other two school VR projects, was very much at an early stage of
its development. Nevertheless, as in the other two projects, the
school's staff felt that the VR system could enhance learning, not only
by giving pupils a sense of control, but also by allowing them to gain
self-confidence by using sophisticated technology. In the case of the
Shepherd School, as in the others, a type of collaborative learning
emerged. As one of the researchers on the project noted, "one of the
most powerful uses of the learning aid developed spontaneously.
Older and more able students began to help and guide younger and
less able students through each level, encouraging them to say and
sign the word when encountering each new symbol" (Brown
1993:12).

In contrast to what occurred in the other school projects, in the
Shepherd School project it was possible to identify specific technical
difficulties in using the VR system. The main problem many pupils

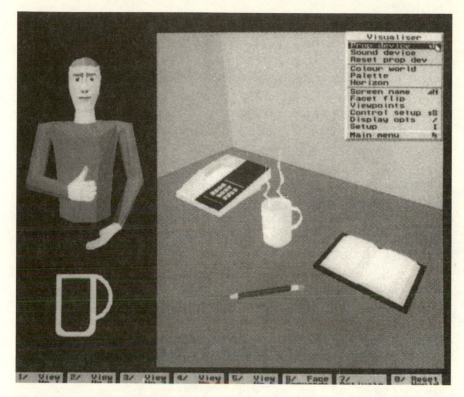

Figure 4.4   A Deskworld for learning the word "mug."

encountered was difficulty navigating with the spaceball and the mouse. But unlike with other VR problems such as disorientation and display resolution, which can only be resolved in the longer term, it has been possible to work toward resolving the navigation shortcoming by making use of a stationary joystick (see Figure 4.3). It has also been possible to improve the system by making the layout of the screen more user-friendly (see Figure 4.4).

More generally, what is interesting here is that the VR system—or more specifically, the system's ability to manipulate objects in a three-dimensional world—has supported the particular approach to learning on which the Makaton system is based: namely, one that tries to develop communication skills by building a sense of the relationship between real world objects and language. This is a feature of VR that may apply beyond the special needs context.[12]

Pupils in all three schools clearly enjoyed the sense of independence and achievement that comes from constructing and being able to manipulate virtual worlds. But apart from this, some specific advantages and shortcomings of VR use can be identified in each setting. The success of the Shepherd School's project, for example, has much to do with the fact that the skills learned are of direct practical use— namely, pupils acquire language skills that are tailored to meet their needs at particular stages of learning. This provides an important contrast with West Denton's Dangerous Workplace. Although pupils there learned much about design and about computing, only a few of them (those who worked in conjunction with NEI Parsons) were able to relate the virtual environment to the real-life situation on the factory floor. Even if they were able to make the connection, it is difficult to see how they could relate the skill of designing a safe machine tool or forklift to their broader educational experience. It is therefore important to think about the relationship between the use of VR and the skills and contexts for which it will be relevant.

One way to test the skills that have been acquired with VR, incidentally, is by testing them in the real world. This is one direction in which the VIRART collaboration with the Shepherd School has subsequently gone. The VIRART team has since created virtual worlds for developing shopping and traffic safety skills, and one way to test the effectiveness of their application is to see whether users' skills have improved in the real world after some practice in the virtual world (Brown, Cobb, and Eastgate 1994).

Similarly, at the Oregon Research Institute, trials are under way to teach wheelchair-bound children traffic safety skills in virtual worlds, and again, the results are measured against performance in the real world (Buckert-Donelson 1995). But what needs to be pointed out in cases in which pupils learn "real-world" skills by practicing them in virtual worlds is that the benefits specific to VR technology do not necessarily reflect on the "realism" achieved by the VR system or on the closeness between the virtual world and the real one. Instead, tests of the skills pupils have learned are more likely to shed light on the usefulness of the equipment and on the success of the teaching methods.

Developers of VR technology have argued, particularly in trying to demonstrate the benefits of the technology, that the closer VR comes to emulating real-world tasks or the more VR is able to represent "realistic" virtual worlds, the more users will gain from the technology. This argument is made to counter what is regarded as the more frivolous side of VR, such as the fantasy worlds of VR games or the more farfetched ideas about VR applications. It is true that VR applications that make use of VR to visualize real-life phenomena, in architecture or medicine for example, have shown themselves to be useful in relation to the realism they achieve. But the same may not apply in education where, as we have seen, the capacity for world-building and for exploring interactive worlds has proved particularly worthwhile.

Hence, too, other applications of VR in education that have not been discussed here, such as teaching mathematics (Winn and Bricken 1992) and physics (Aukstakalnis and Blatner 1992: 218–219), have exploited the fact that VR can help to explore worlds that cannot be explored by other means (see also Gay 1994). Since the way in which VR technology is used for teaching and learning is far from settled, we will want to keep in mind the diversity of how the technology can be used.

The experience at West Denton High School indicates that the link between the real-world setting and the design of the virtual world was the least successful aspect of this VR project. But this may stem from the fact that VR so far has not been widely used in relation to the workaday world. The ease of world-building and the ability to explore VR itself, however—as in the case of the HITLab summer school—proved to be very rewarding for pupils, who, again, benefited from the fact that learning how to build virtual worlds, unlike other skills, takes such a short time.

It should be added that these benefits from VR relate not so much to learning about individual aspects of design, as might be the case with skills acquired in a computer-aided-design course, but rather from getting a sense of being able to construct whole virtual worlds and the ability to explore and manipulate them. The benefits of the VR project at the Shepherd School, finally, which did not involve world-building on the part of pupils, were nevertheless such that they related to the specific advantages of VR technology—in this case, exercising control over the virtual world and how this control was integrated in the learning process itself.

VR applications for training purposes can be briefly mentioned here for the sake of comparison. Training applications have exploited VR technology in one of two ways: they have either used a virtual environment to avoid the dangers of training in real-world settings, in such applications as battlefield simulations (Stytz 1994) and tasks relating to hazardous situations (for example, Stone 1994:54–55). The most important advantage to be gained from VR here is the cost-effectiveness of carrying out the training in a virtual world rather than in the real one. In training applications such as these, however, VR is competing against a number of other tools that may not provide presence or interaction, but that may be less expensive.

The second type of VR training applications have taken advantage of immersing a number of users in the same environment, in other words, in shared virtual worlds (the VIRTUOSI project and SIM-NET, which were mentioned in Chapters 2 and 3, are good examples). But in shared virtual worlds, it is not clear whether the benefit lies with VR technology specifically or with the ability to bring a number of users together. Perhaps these shared virtual world applications should be classed with networked simulations or with teleoperations rather than VR. Thus it remains to be seen how closely VR comes to be associated with training. It is nevertheless clear that the benefits and disadvantages of VR in relation to training can be separated from those of VR in the classroom.

Put differently, the uses of VR in education occupy a distinct niche, and this niche may not be the one that relates most closely to VR development in other areas, such as scientific visualization or entertainment. The specific advantages of VR in the projects discussed here range from creating a sense of movement and control within an environment where there may be restrictions on them to creating worlds of play and of the imagination that are possible only within artificial or simulated worlds.

Drawing lessons from the three VR settings allows us to begin putting VR in education into a larger context. At the moment, it looks as though other VR applications, especially entertainment, will eclipse the use of VR in education. But as we shall explain in the following section, the kinds of virtual worlds that have been developed for entertainment purposes have so far largely followed the content and the format of existing computer games and arcade simulator games. Moreover, the possibilities for interaction with the virtual world, or more specifically for exploring the environment in any depth, have been very limited in VR games.

Even if VR games come to provide experiences of a relatively high technical standard, so far they have not capitalized on what are perhaps the most distinctive capabilities of VR systems—being able to build virtual worlds of one's own design and manipulate them.[13] In short, entertainment games have not yet fully been able to exploit the unique features of VR technology in the same way that educational uses have. This is important because the way VR systems come to be used depends not only on the technical qualities of the systems, but on the momentum that particular uses of the technology achieve in different application contexts.

Adventures in Cyberspace

It's you, in there. (Jonathan Waldern)[14]

Games have become the most popular and well-known application of VR. Jonathan Waldern, founder of W Industries, the company that produced the first immersive VR game system, announced in April 1993 that more than three million people had used his company's games.[15] At that time, the technology had just begun to emerge and Waldern's games were the only immersive VR systems available to the public. Since then, a number of games systems have become available and games are the most likely way the public will come into contact with VR.

As in the case of the makers and vendors of personal computers, many VR developers and manufacturers have distanced themselves from games applications of VR because they feel that it is not "serious."[16] It is also interesting to note that the label "virtual reality" only became attached to Waldern's W Industries game after the term had become popularized by Jaron Lanier. Waldern, who had been working on 3-D computer display technology for over ten years, launched his first games in 1990–1991, just as Lanier began drawing media attention to the new technology. This publicity prompted Waldern to attach the label "virtual reality" to his games machines (*Black Ice* 1993:16).[17] His firm, W Industries, has since changed its name to Virtuality.

We can begin with Virtuality, since the company's VR games were the first on the consumer market and are still the most popular arcade games.[18] A Virtuality game consists of a head-mounted display system and a "flying" joystick control when it is configured as a stand-up game. When it is a sit-down game, it comes with a stationary joystick. Inside his or her helmet, the player sees and hears a three-dimensional world and navigates and shoots by means of the joystick control.

Virtuality games are therefore similar (except for the flying joystick) to the immersive VR systems produced by Lanier's VPL in 1989–1991, although the technical specifications of the two systems are quite different. Another difference between the Virtuality games and the VPL systems—both of which, again, gained popularity at around the same time—is that the VPL systems were expressly designed to facilitate *creating* virtual worlds. This was also one of the features of VR that caught the public's imagination (Lanier and Biocca 1993:151–152). The world of the Virtuality games, by contrast, is ready-made. In this respect, Virtuality games are similar to other computer and video games, and they also share the same genres, such as flight simulation, shoot-'em-ups, and the like.

VR games often combine existing computer-game formats with some novel elements. For example, the content of the Virtuality multiplayer game Legend Quest (see Figure 5.1) borrows many features from conventional dungeons and dragons games. Players choose from among several characters and perform various tasks within a series of interconnected rooms, moving from easier to more difficult levels of play. What makes the virtual reality version of this game so appealing by comparison with, say, a board game version, is the sense of immersion combined with the narrative content. Here, for example, is one player's description of Legend Quest: "You forget where you are. You actually feel like you're in that dungeon and fighting. You panic. If something starts killing you, you try and get away. There are some rooms I dread going back to." According to another player: "In Virtual Reality, you're not controlling a character. You are the character. The interaction is brain to brain, person to person. It's just the visual aspect of the person that's different."[19] It seems, then, that the "realism" of the game and the ability to interact with other users within the virtual world sets VR games apart from others, although, as we shall see in more detail in the next chapter, the notion of "realism" is not as simple as it seems.

It is interesting to compare these abovementioned players' reactions to those of a VR researcher: Warren Robinett has been a successful developer of computer games as well as a highly regarded VR researcher at the University of North Carolina at Chapel Hill. On the occasion of his first encounter with Virtuality's stand-up game Dactyl Nightmare, he immediately explored the display standard and navigational flexibility of the machine. He moved his helmeted head and the joystick vigorously in order to discover the responsiveness of the tracking device and the way the virtual world could be navigated. Unlike other users, he was not interested in the content of game, but was clearly impressed with the machine's technical capabilities.[20] The distinction between the technical aspects of the machine and the content of the virtual world is one that we shall return to in the next chapter, but it is noteworthy that Robinett, an "expert" who was familiar with the most advanced VR systems at the time, considered the first generation of immersive VR games to be of a high technical standard.

Robinett's response, in turn, can be compared with the responses to a different, nonimmersive game called Mandala. This games machine, developed by Vincent John Vincent, is not immersive but similar to Myron Krueger's "artificial reality." The Mandala game uses a video-camera to record a silhouette of the user that can then interact with the image of a virtual environment displayed on a screen, which may be television-sized or larger. The games that can be played include a virtual drum kit that allows the user to play the instruments on the screen, ball games, and interactive dance routines. These games are often used by two or more users since participants are able to step directly into the environment (i.e., they do not have to put on an HMD or other tracking devices). The machine that runs Mandala consists of several low-cost components, and it is possible for an amateur to learn how to program the system to create different environments and sound effects and to reconfigure the elements of the system.

The differences between the reaction of users to their first encounter with Mandala compared with the reactions of those using an immersive VR system are revealing: Mandala users express delight at immediately being able to "play" music, for example, or to play ball in the virtual environment. The Mandala system allows for a form of interaction that can be grasped quickly and intuitively, and the focus is immediately on the interaction. Hence interaction—rather than "realism"—is the key to the appeal of the game. The differences between Dactyl Nightmare and Mandala are reflected in the aims of their creators. Waldern is explicit about the type of experiences that Virtuality aims to provide: The "ideology of total immersion is what we're focused on."[21] A leaflet advertising Mandala VR systems, by contrast, talks of "real time interactive experiences."

Users are not very impressed with the technology of the Mandala system, which is more like technologies they are already familiar with, such as video-recording, computer games, and synthesized music. The reactions to immersive environments, in comparison, typically focus on the novelty of the technology. Users of the latter are often disoriented by their first immersive experience and are disappointed by the quality of the display but express amazement at the new technology. Simply put, users consider immersive VR technically impressive, whereas the Mandala systems are more fun.[22]

The same applies to the multiuser versions of the two types of games: Mandala gives two or more users the sense that they are interacting within another environment, whereas with Virtuality, as we shall see later, it is difficult to become accustomed to the "presence" of another player. This is partly because in Virtuality games, the user does not have a chance to become used to interacting with the virtual environment or with other players, because the games usually last only a few minutes. The economics of "throughput" (the number of players that the machine needs to be able to handle in a short period of time in order to make a profit) in arcade games do not permit longer games, whereas with the Mandala game, part of the appeal is that the sense of interaction can be achieved very quickly.

At this point, we can broaden the discussion to look at the relation between Virtuality games and other computer games. In many ways, Virtuality games are like conventional arcade and computer-based games. Like other coin-operated arcade games, they are sold as complete units and designed in a robust manner so that they can be used in public spaces. New Virtuality software can be loaded onto arcade units, which makes these games similar to other computer games in that the manufacturer's profit is accrued not only from the sale of the machines but from the subsequent sale of new games to the arcade operators.

In terms of content, too, Virtuality games follow existing computer games.[23] They are mainly "action" adventures, with an emphasis on speed and violence. The second generation of Virtuality games, released in 1994, added virtual boxing, which has been one of the most popular formats for screen-based arcade and home computer games. Another new game, Zonehunter, features android-style warriors (see Figure 4.5).

In Zonehunter, the player "becomes" an androidlike warrior equipped with a powerful weapon for killing alien creatures and other players. And again, like other arcade and computer games, Zonehunter owes much to popular Hollywood films such as *Robocop,* *Aliens,* and *Terminator.* The thudding steps of the figure, throbbing sound effects, and dramatic "realism" of the explosions are all de-

Figure 4.5   Three people playing the Virtuality game Zonehunter.

signed to reinforce this impression. Such a link between popular film and television programs and computer games has become an important marketing strategy for games manufacturers. Finally, this second generation of Virtuality games has also been technically improved and features a lighter HMD and more "realistic" texture-mapped computer graphics.

It might be said that VR technology is being used here to deliver content from another medium and make it appealing by other means. This, again, is a typical pattern for consumer electronics entertainment, as the case of multimedia personal computers demonstrates (Silverstone and Haddon 1993). Virtuality machines seem to be designed to amplify the type of experience that is already possible with other, existing technologies.

Meanwhile, non-VR computer games have been using ever more "realistic" computer graphics and more compelling types of interaction. But VR games technology also takes these realistic effects and the interaction with the game to new levels. Conversely, VR games do not exploit the features that are unique to this as opposed to other entertainment technologies, such as creating or exploring virtual worlds. It needs to be added here that the fact that VR games follow the format of existing computer games is closely related to the economics of arcade games, which need to offer a short and highly engrossing experience. Whether, once they are used in the home, VR games continue to follow this format remains to be seen.

Even if entertainment uses of VR are only just beginning to gain momentum, it may still be useful to look briefly at some similar technologies that are used for entertainment. As we have seen, VR systems have been mainly designed for single users, although an increasing number of projects are exploring networked VR. One comparable technology that comes to mind is television, which is the principal form of leisure in advanced societies. Two features of television may be particularly relevant: one is that although people spend more time watching television than pursuing any other form of leisure, this activity does not rate very highly in terms of satisfaction (Argyle 1992:106). In fact, on such a scale, it is rated among the least satisfying pursuits. This could be relevant to the entertainment uses of VR inasmuch as it is widely believed that in the future, television may become interactive or may take the form of a multimedia device that combines television with some of the capabilities of personal computers and telecommunications.

It is still not clear, however, whether interactive media will be the wave of the future. Research emerging from past interactive television projects shows that the use of these services has been disappointing (Rogers 1986:62–64 and passim). Moreover, as Neumann (1991) has argued, audience habits are likely to change very slowly; interactivity may only develop gradually and there may be less demand for it than might be expected. In this connection, it is worth mentioning a recent pilot study of networked households that were offered a range of interactive services. Out of the wide range of services offered, the only significant demand for networked interactive multimedia was for games. People wanted their households hooked up so that they could play games with each other.[24]

Networked computer games, too, seem to be more appealing to players than the stand-alone versions of the same games. At many VR labs and firms, for example, playing networked computer games—sometimes with 3-D perspectives, like the recent game DOOM—is a popular pastime among employees (see also Giles 1994). In one sense, this is not surprising since these institutions are equipped with access to high-speed networked computers. What is perhaps surprising—or revealing—is that people who spend a lot of time working with VR and with computers also choose to spend their leisure time with them.

A different picture emerges when we draw on the experience of players of conventional computer games. This technology offers an important comparison with VR games since, as mentioned earlier, various HMDs for home use are now being marketed and other such VR systems have been promised for the near future.

The size of the computer games industry is substantial. It has been estimated that in 1991, Americans spent $10 billion on "interactive entertainment," $7 billion of which was spent on arcade games and the remaining $3 billion on computer games (Stefanac 1993:40). Another recent study of computer games has put global sales of (nonarcade) computer games at $4 billion in 1990, a market that is dominated by Sega and Nintendo (Provenzo 1991:8). Mackay cites figures of between 50 percent and 33 percent market penetration for computer games in the United States and Japan, with the U.K. behind at 15 percent (1995:336). Even in the U.K., however, computer games have in recent years accounted for more than half of all toy sales (Kay 1994).

The British market for computer games is overwhelmingly male (80 percent), and ownership of computer games is highest among the youngsters, including teenagers, followed by the 35- to 44-year-old group.[25] Nintendo of America initially targeted the male population aged between 8 and 15, "the traditional heavy users," but later found that "the biggest group of primary users continues to be boys in that 8 to 11 group, accounting for about 36 percent of our total users, and the second biggest group, just a point and a half behind that, are adults 18 plus."[26] Apart from gender and age differences, there seem to be no clear patterns in socioeconomic terms for computer game ownership, at least in the U.K.[27]

The market for location-based entertainment games is also considerable. The Virtual World Entertainment game Battletech, for example, which is a desktop VR game played in networked capsules, sold over 30,000 tickets in Tokyo within the first month of operation (early 1993); in the United States the total was almost 350,000 for 1993 (Sprout 1993:20). In this market, however, VR games are competing with other highly sophisticated games, such as those featuring motion platforms as well as simulator-type games. These games change rapidly to meet the ever higher expectations of customers. The Sega R-360 flight simulator capsule, for example, involves a jet-fighter battle that spins the user through 360 degrees at a stomach-churning pace.

The characteristics of VR arcade games are currently closest to those of location-based simulator games and other arcade games. There is an important difference, however, between the direct experience of an environment using VR technology and the experience of an environment using simulator technology: VR players are completely shut off by an HMD, and in multiplayer games, two or more players directly experience the same environment. There is also a difference in terms of input, inasmuch as the player's input is transmitted via head-mounted tracking and navigation by means of a flying joystick. The differences in content among VR games and other arcade and simulator games are more difficult to pinpoint, but VR games tend to emphasize the three-dimensional spaces in which the action takes place.

At this stage, we can return to the comparison between VR and home computer games—a comparison that, again, is particularly important in light of the potential market for home VR games. Computer games can, of course, also be played in arcades, but in arcade games, the duration of play is limited by financial considerations. In the home, once a game has been purchased, this constraint does not apply.[28]

VR, as we have seen, involves presence in—and interaction with—a computer-generated environment. Therefore, one question that we can ask is: To what extent do other home computer games approximate this kind of experience? To approach the issue indirectly, we can ask first to what extent players are oblivious to the environment around them. It is obvious that although players are engaged in play, they can still be aware of and respond to changes around them. Here the parallel can be drawn to the behavior of someone watching television; studies have shown that people watching TV are not necessarily "absorbed" by programs, but may be doing other things at the same time. People behave similarly when playing computer games.

But instead of looking at computer games from the point of view of research findings, let us take a concrete example: During an afternoon of observing four children playing computer games in the living room of a London family, I noted that parents came and went, there were

eating and drinking breaks, conversations between players and with
bystanders, and so on. In short, games play did not bring the social
world to a standstill; or, to put it differently, everyday life continued
to circulate in and out of the activities of players. *But* (and here the
differences between games and television begin to come into focus),
the games continued for more than four hours. Apart from the breaks
between different levels of play and breaks between games themselves, both of which typically lasted less than half a minute, play was
nonstop. Moreover, the narrative of the games was such that visual
attention could only be broken off for seconds and players tended to
speak only in brief spurts. The game music (or "jingle") was also constant, including during changes of level, and had a rhythm that was
synchronized to amplify the intensity of the game's narrative. In
other words, within the orbit of the screen, the console, and the
player, the attention paid to the game was practically uninterrupted.[29]

A different approach to computer games might be to ask, to what
extent do players identify with the game? One way of answering this
question is to give some examples of how players speak while playing.
Here are sample utterances taken from the afternoon mentioned previously, during which four children played the popular Sonic the
Hedgehog game, which features a blue hedgehog who chases
through different landscapes performing tasks: "Now I've become
supersonic" (i.e., obtained additional powers); "I can turn into a
ring"; "Now I can collect the ring"; "You've killed it"; and "Move
over." Assuming the role of a blue hedgehog in first-person speech
does not rule out third-person forms of speech: for example, "Here
you need to collect the rings" and "What does the special move do
here?" Another type of identification is with the character's body:
when a character is being punched or takes a steep fall, for example,
players will often twitch or make other "sympathetic" movements.
Except for these movements and the use of both hands for the joystick controls, players remain motionless. When two players are playing, the relation between the two on-screen characters mainly consists
of keeping up with each other and coordinating movements.

Identification with a screen character is not the only way to achieve
interaction in a computer game. Some games involve the player in a
more "direct" way. The game Wolfenstein 3-D, for example, gives
players a direct perspective on a three-dimensional world on the
screen. Here, players have an on-screen control panel on the bottom
of the screen as well as using the joystick to "move" the perspective of

the player through a series of rooms. The object of Wolfenstein is to kill Nazis and their guard dogs and perform various other tasks, such as collecting more ammunition. The three-dimensional effect and texture-mapped computer graphics give the game a realistic appearance. "Realism," however, does not feature in all computer games. One computer game that does not use on-screen characters, for example, is SimCity, a game that allows players to create a three-dimensional image of a city and simulate its workings, which includes experiencing municipal politics and the transport system, and creating the newspaper. Wolfenstein and SimCity are only two illustrations of the forms the involvement of players in computer games can take.

There are various other ways of analyzing players' involvement in computer games. One is to draw on the literature about the spectator's activity in film and television narratives (Provenzo 1991). Or it might be possible to look at the various social roles adopted off-screen. Haddon, for example, found in relation to computer games that "certain boys were identified as self-styled experts," whereas others adopted a more apprenticelike role (1992:88). Another way to analyze player involvement might be to look at the on-screen role models, such as the superhero or the streetfighter. Whatever such analyses might yield, one of the differences between VR and other computer games is that involvement is likely to be intensified in an immersive VR game, since there are almost no cues from the environment outside the HMD.

Against this background of conventional computer games, we can now turn to VR games for household consumption. It is still too early to estimate the popularity of these games or to speculate about possible patterns of use, since only a few HMDs and VR software tools have so far come onto the market. Still, several features of these components and of the VR systems that have been announced stand out: the first is that these games feature an HMD with modest technical specifications, plus a joystick or hand-controller with push buttons. The HMDs tend to be lightweight and offer low-resolution graphics. The position-tracking, though not accurate compared with that of advanced systems, is acceptable for the tasks required by the games. The content and software are similar to that of existing computer games, except that the VR games exploit the ability to navigate in a three-dimensional space more fully. In at least one case, software for the creation of virtual worlds is among the options available, but whether this use of the technology will become popular remains to be seen.

Be that as it may, in most VR games, interaction, again, is similar to interaction in other computer games: shooting creatures and the like and being taken through levels of increasing skill and difficulty. At the same time, the cost of VR games is now approaching the standard price of other home computer games. And although the games may therefore not "push" the technical specifications of VR systems in the way that laboratories and high-end applications do, VR games technology has congealed into a particular shape and has achieved a price-performance ratio similar to that of other consumer electronics devices. This is the shape of VR technology as it prepares to seek a market in the home.

In considering the possibility of more widespread uses of VR technology, we should briefly examine health and safety issues. The psychological and health problems related to VR fall outside the scope of this study and they are outside the realm of my competence. Thus, my main concern will be with the social aspects surrounding health and safety rather than health and safety issues per se.

Concerns over health and safety can be divided into those that are not specific to VR systems, such as the hygiene of location-based entertainment systems (the spread of bacteria can be a major problem in an HMD worn by many users), and VR-specific issues such as eyestrain.[30] Among researchers, the issues surrounding VR are often discussed under the heading of simulator sickness, since most of the available studies have dealt with flight simulators.[31] For our purposes, it will suffice to say here that this research continues to generate controversy, that the research that has been done on VR is still in its infancy, and that apart from those who have a vested interest in claiming that VR systems are safe to use, many researchers, including those just cited, agree that too little is known about the effects of VR to draw any firm conclusions.

Two findings from the research on simulator sickness are worth singling out. The first is that there seem to be considerable differences in the degree to which different groups of people are prone to simulation sickness, depending, for example, on age (Biocca 1992a: 338–340). The second shows that the increased "realism" of virtual worlds may increase rather than diminish some simulator sickness effects (Biocca 1992a:341). The significance of these findings, as

Biocca points out in an essay entitled "Will Simulation Sickness Slow Down the Diffusion of Virtual Environment Technology?" is that problems with VR are unlikely to go away, if only because a number of uncertainties are likely to remain even if the technology improves dramatically.[32]

The problems of eyestrain and the psychological effects of VR may or may not be connected, but eyestrain is more easily measurable (see Kalawsky 1993). Here we should recall that VR is primarily a visual tool and that innovation in display technology, whether for television, for computing, or for VR, has been advancing rapidly. The trade-off between cost and the fidelity of the visual display, which is often mentioned in discussions about the future of VR, is therefore constantly changing.

Another problem concerns the aftereffects of VR use. One solution that has been suggested for this are "cooling-off periods." If, for example, after spending lots of time using a VR system, the user wants to drive a car, a certain period of rest ought to be allowed first for regaining a sense of the real world. Yet irrespective of whether this "cooling off" would address the problems associated with extensive VR use, this kind of "remedy" could imply that VR is similar to alcohol or drug abuse and might therefore create additional public anxiety with regard to VR technology. We should also remind ourselves that one of the reasons why VR health and safety issues have so far not resulted in a "moral panic"[33] is that VR systems outside of laboratories, until now, have been used only for short periods. This would almost certainly change with VR games that can be used at home.

New technologies often arouse anxieties. An important precedent here is the strong reaction to the sudden popularity of computer games (or, going further back, to the introduction of television). Computer games enjoyed a long period of popularity among computer enthusiasts before they became a commercial success. When millions were sold in the early 1980s, however, there was a sudden public outcry. Parents worried that their children would become "addicted" to these games and the media devoted considerable attention to the subject. When the computer game boom subsided in the mid-1980s, so, too, did the fears and the media attention. More recently, the boom in sales of console computer games in the early 1990s started a similar outcry that has, again, faded from view.

Among the causes for reactions against new technologies, according to Shotton (1989), is fear triggered when they suddenly become widespread. The personal computer had only just moved into the home when computer games became popular. In the past, Shotton points out, technologies like the automobile were introduced much more slowly and still aroused anxieties. VR has moved from being unknown to being widely known in a very short time, mainly in the form of games. In addition to the impression that VR is an uncontrollable technology, there may also be fear that it somehow threatens to distort "reality," however distant this prospect may seem with the present technology.

We can distinguish among several specific concerns, apart from the general anxiety about children or young people spending time with an "unknown" technology: the supposed "druglike" quality of VR and the possibility that it may lead to social dysfunctionality; the question of long-term use or dependency; the "deviance" or "delinquency" associated with the games arcade; and the worry about the effects of violent or pornographic uses of VR.

As regards the concern over addiction, the closest parallel is computer addiction, which has been extensively discussed by Shotton (1989). She concluded that even if some computer users could be identified as being "dependent" on computers, there has been no evidence to suggest that this dependency is crucially reinforced by computers or by computer technology per se, or that it has any long-term ill effects. "Dependents" are to be found mainly among those who may be predisposed to spending time with inanimate objects or to seek pleasure in solitary activities anyway. In terms of the association of arcades with deviance and the like, the operators of arcades have responded by providing a more family-oriented atmosphere in many venues or restyling the arcades as themed entertainment centers.

The issues of violence and pornography have recently come to the fore again thanks to advanced computer graphics in games and material that is considered pornographic on the Internet. It is likely (if previous waves of moral panic are anything to go by) that these public concerns will fade as the technology is no longer perceived as being new. However, it is difficult to imagine that the health and safety studies currently under way could come to the kinds of conclusions that would reassure the public concerning the dangers of VR. Hence it seems that VR will continue to be the subject of well-founded concerns as well as sporadic moral panics.[34]

Until now, VR games have mainly been used in arcades and theme parks, and the market for home VR games is still in its infancy.[35] Recently, however, a number of HMDs, such as Virtual I/O's (see Figure 2.2), have become available that are designed for use with personal computers and priced for the home market. The manufacturers who have begun to offer low-cost HMDs and VR games software have so far mostly been smaller firms. Nevertheless, several home VR systems produced by larger manufacturers are poised to come onto the market in the near future. Sega, for example, has signed collaborative agreements with Virtuality to develop a home VR game with an HMD (Sega already offers an arcade VR game in Yokohama called VR-1 Space Mission. See Figure 3.4). Another collaboration between Virtuality and the computer games company Atari has announced an inexpensive home VR game for 1996. Nintendo is not far behind. It has teamed up with Silicon Graphics, a firm that, as we saw earlier, has extensive computer graphics and VR-related experience, in a venture code-named Project Reality. Nintendo already sells a monochromatic VR game called Virtual Boy, which can also be rented in video rental stores.

Since VR games have become the most popular application of VR, it may be useful to widen our horizons at this point and consider the broader implications of this form of leisure. We can do this by briefly looking at some relevant insights from a number of disciplines, beginning with media and communications studies. One approach that has recently been adopted in this field has been to champion the cause of the active audience or of the active participant in popular culture—with the implication that the audience's activity should somehow be seen not as a passive pursuit but as an enabling one.

Interactive technologies might seem to be a particularly good example of this kind of active engagement. But a discussion of active participation can only lead to the question of whether new communication technologies, and perhaps VR, should be seen as "active" pursuits. In any case, the criticisms that have been made of the "active audience" approach suggest that the notion of the "activity" of the spectator is problematic. Silverstone, for example, has argued that "the key issue is not so much whether an audience is active but whether that activity is significant" (1994:153).[36]

These question marks about "active" participation should not lead us immediately to the notion that VR game players should be regarded as passive "helmet potatoes" (to make an analogy with televisual "couch potatoes"). As we have seen, the demand for VR may not be linked so much to content, but to the fact that it is a new technology. A desire for new experiences per se, Campbell has argued, is central to modern consumer culture. Moreover, consumerism is not, as is often thought, imposed on the individual from the outside, but rather involves an "autonomous imaginative hedonism" (1987:77) that restlessly seeks to experience the new.[37] The allegedly unbounded possibilities of virtual worlds—which are in fact, as we have seen, subject to both technological and social constraints—could conceivably go some way toward explaining the enthusiasm for VR games.

Such an explanation would, nevertheless, have to be placed in a broader context of changing patterns of consumer behavior in relation to new information and communication technologies (ICTs). Hence we could go on to ask, for example, whether the popularity of interactive games and of interactive entertainment represents a shift away from the consumption of more passive experiences of ICTs. Mackay thinks so:

> The interactive nature of computer games is clearly central to their enormous popularity. The growth of such media, together with falling television audiences, would suggest consumer demand for interactivity, for a changed relationship between producer and audience . . . the scale and significance of this shift should not be underestimated: for a whole generation, video games have superseded popular music as the main form of entertainment. (1995:336)

But this demand for interactivity implies that there is a strong contrast between the active nature of these games and the "passive leisure" of television (Mackay 1995:338). The question then becomes whether such a sharp distinction can be made between the two. In the case of multimedia, for instance, which should provide a good example of the demand for interactivity, Silverstone and Haddon are sceptical: "What is not clear is how far multimedia will be seen to be offering a radical new development of interactivity or one that is actually in demand. This is despite the fact that those who develop it, and those potential customers who see it, can identify a qualitatively new media experience" (1993:18). It is also difficult to define interactivity: "Interactivity . . . has at least two principal dimensions. The first is technical—interactivity involves some degree of physical control over what is taking place on the screen . . . [it] is also a psychological concept, and as such it is considerably more problematic" (1993:18).

If interactivity is problematic, so is seeing VR and other computer-based games as passive pursuits. Sorlin, for example, argues that "if we consider people's attitudes, we see that the recreational part of the media triggers more active reactions than their informatory part, which makes it necessary to examine the media within the general framework of enjoyment such as it develops in contemporary societies" (1994:90). This kind of "framework" would take us far beyond the implications of interactive VR games. What Sorlin nevertheless rightly points to is the fact that the issue of the "activity" or "passivity" (or indeed "interactivity") cannot be posed in relation to individual technologies, but must be examined in the wider context of the everyday uses of a range of technologies. It may also be useful to recall here that the kinds of activity that we encountered in the context of educational experiences with VR are different from both the recreational and informatory uses of technology that Sorlin is describing. Or again, the kinds of activity involved in the classroom are different from the activity of playing VR games and computer games.

These differences are particularly important since they raise the issue of the manipulability of virtual worlds (which we shall come back to in the final chapter). One way of pursuing this topic, at this stage, however, is to try to identify what makes VR experiences unique among our existing uses of information and communication technologies, and this is a task to which we can now turn.

5

Virtual Worlds and the Varieties of Interactive Experience

So far, we have looked at the emergence of VR technologies and at some examples of how they have come to be used. At this point, we can begin to consider the social implications of VR technology in a different way: apart from the "local" contexts, we also need to get a sense of the range of ways in which VR technology is being used. This can be done by presenting an inventory of virtual worlds and of their key features.

Apart from looking at content, we must also examine the forms of interaction: what range of interaction is supported by VR systems? As a next step, we can compare this range of interaction with how we can do similar things with other, existing technologies. This comparison will enable us to say how interaction with virtual worlds fits into the landscape of conventional information and communication technologies or how VR departs from existing uses of technologies or reinforces them—and how it therefore, although still in its early stages, is beginning to change the way we use machines and the way we live our everyday lives.

Inside Cyberspace: The Multiuser Game Legend Quest

One way to describe the content of virtual worlds is by giving a (subjective) narrative account of the experience.[1] We can use the game Legend Quest to illustrate what kinds of components a virtual world typically contains and to allow us to identify what kinds of trade-offs are made in the design of virtual worlds. This will also provide a back-drop against which we will be able to make comparisons with the characteristics of other virtual worlds.

Legend Quest is a multiuser dungeons and dragons game, one of a handful of arcade games produced by Virtuality. The games can be played in arcades or in special VR-themed cafés and they feature an HMD and hand-held "flying" joystick.[2] As with other immersive VR worlds, the first impression the Legend Quest world makes on those who step inside is one of disorientation. The first reaction of users is to look around to get a sense of their surroundings, as they would in other virtual worlds or in unfamiliar environments in the real world.

The next step is to move forward by pressing the joystick button. In many other virtual worlds, one of the first things that often happens to users at this point is that they become lost by moving beyond the bounds of the world—either by flying in such a way that they reach a dark area above it, below it, or beyond its farthest horizon. The Legend Quest world, however, is designed so that the player can only move within a limited range of height, from crouching to eye level. And since the virtual world consists of a number of rooms connected by doors, hallways, and stairways, the user experiences little disorientation (apart from not knowing where the rooms will lead) other than the initial sense of dislocation when entering this world. Height constraints, built in to prevent users from becoming "lost" or disoriented, have become an important element of virtual world design, especially for worlds intended for novice users.

After the user becomes acclimatized to his or her surroundings, he or she feels immersed in the virtual world, although interruptions, mainly in the form of noises from the world outside the VR system, penetrate the user's awareness. From this point on, the experience of immersion is reinforced by the game tasks that now have to be fulfilled. What does this world look and sound like, once the game tasks begin? The appearance of the virtual world has much in common with an animated film—it includes boxlike rooms, creatures, and objects made up of primary-colored, angular, shaded planes (see Figure 5.1).

Virtual worlds often look like animated films, although this similarity has not received much comment. In a sense, this similarity is a matter of degree, since shading and lighting, for example, can give virtual worlds a more photo-realistic rather than a cartoonlike appearance. This similarity is, nevertheless, an important feature because if

Figure 5.1   Fighting against a skeleton in Legend Quest.

we ask why, once inside a cartoonlike environment, users are able to suspend disbelief and treat such an environment as if they were in the real world, one immediate answer that suggests itself is that we are used to the conventions of animated films.

The Legend Quest rooms are boxlike in the sense that they are made up of flat and single-colored planes, some with a brick pattern. Occasionally there are other details on the walls, like lamps or pictures. The objects in the rooms are few and rudimentary: treasure chests that can be opened, candles, fires, doors that can be opened by means of door-handles and keys, and the like. Finally, there are the creatures, such as elves, maidens, skeletons, wolves, and bats, all cartoonlike in appearance and in their "behaviors." Again, the user quickly becomes used to this environment in order to concentrate on killing these creatures and fulfilling other tasks.

We must also briefly mention sound. Inside the world, there are several types of sound: the voice-over (like the voice-over in a film), which occasionally provides the narrative of the game, announcing, for instance, the impending end of the game ("Time to die," intones a deep, droning male voice); brief spurts of music at the beginning and end of the game; the sound of one's own footsteps, which seem to echo in the room; the voice of the fellow player (if the game is played in multiuser mode), and the sounds made by other creatures (bat shrieks, skeleton laughs, wolf howls, and so on). Again, the "strangeness" of these sounds fades away quickly, although the voice-over remains disconcerting, since it refers to something "outside" the world. The user is likely to concentrate on the other player's voice more than on other noises, since the voice is the most familiar sound in an otherwise strange environment (although since the voice is modulated to suit the character adopted by the player—for instance, a high-pitched voice for an elf—the coplayer's voice remains somewhat alien).

The other player in the Legend Quest world also adopts a particular character—such as a dwarf, an elf, a warrior, a wizard, or a human—by selecting it before the game begins. A maximum of four players can play. The game also permits selection of particular attributes, such as gender, hair color, and the like. This gives players the appearance of creatures in an animated film. The only part of their own bodies that users can see, however, is their virtual arm. Finding out about one's own appearance is only possible by asking the other player. In any case, the appearance of other players is not of major importance since the user will be mainly aware of others in terms of how they contribute to the task at hand, such as fighting against a skeleton or trying to coordinate what to do next. If players are in different rooms, they will try to locate each other by listening for the other's voice or by looking for each other.

The principal manner in which the other player thus impinges on one's awareness is in relation to one's own position and in coordinating one's movements and actions with the other player's. In Legend Quest's virtual world, there is very little sense of being able to *do* things with one's coplayer. This feeling of not being able to do things with the other player in the virtual environment may be a function of the fact that in our experience of interaction with others in the real world, communication depends, to a great extent, on subtle facial expressions.[3] According to the manufacturer, players on Virtuality machines will soon be able to have photographs of their faces imported into the virtual world. This feature is likely to change the sense one has of the other player and of one's own identity. In any case, in existing games, it is often awkward to have to coordinate one's virtual body in relation to the virtual body of the other player, especially when your virtual bodies are very close to each other. At the same time, the sense that someone else is "there" in the virtual world and of coordinating tasks with the other player, especially after getting used to it, adds significantly to the sensation of being in another world.

Players navigate in the Legend Quest world by means of a hand-held joystick. They point the arm in the direction they wish to travel and press the button used for movement with a thumb. This mode of navigation is intuitively easy, since other familiar devices, such as a computer mouse or the gear shift of a car, operate similarly. The same familiarity applies to operating, by means of a push button, the various weapons, such as swords, daggers, bows, and axes.

With regard to navigation itself, it is noticeable that the sound of one's footsteps does not enhance the sense of motion. That sound seems more a part of the clutter of noises in the Legend Quest world. Thus, navigation is a visual phenomenon. The user moves around naturally by means of a joystick, readily "walking" around, and is drawn to exploring the spaces and paths that are available. This kind of navigation, however "natural," is very different from that used in other virtual reality systems, such as those that allow the user to fly through the virtual world or those in which the user has a whole virtual body (as opposed to having merely a virtual arm, as in this case).

Before we compare Legend Quest's world with other virtual worlds, we can briefly sum up its characteristic features: the world is immersive to the extent that the user's attention is constantly engaged in exploring and interacting with objects and with the other player, mainly in order to keep up with the flow of the tasks at hand. Interestingly, the fact that so much depends on the way in which the tasks are organized around a narrative immediately suggests that one way of making sense of the user's experience is not so much in terms, for example, of the "realism" of the environment, but rather in terms of the narrative of film.[4]

A different way of characterizing the compelling nature of the virtual environment is by noting that when players take off the HMD, the real world seems strange (single games typically last less than five minutes, although purchase of additional time or extended play as a reward for task completion can make games last up to thirty minutes or longer). This postgame readjustment reinforces not so much that the virtual world is "realistic" but that, once inside the virtual world, the user comes to take its "worldlikeness" for granted, despite the fact that it has the appearance of an animated film.

Perhaps the Legend Quest world is compelling, in large part, because of its similarity to other, non-VR computer game worlds. Yet, there are other virtual environments with greater degrees of "realism" and of interaction that are less compelling than Legend Quest—and vice versa (although this may depend on what users are familiar with). The fact that Legend Quest's virtual world is designed for entertainment, or that it has a greater narrative element than other VR experiences, can therefore only partly account for how immersive an experience it provides.

Another of Legend Quest's features that has been highlighted is the absence of a sense of interaction with the other user. Here, comparisons might be made with other technologically-mediated forms of interaction, such as text-based computer-mediated communication, multiplayer computer games, and others. At this point, let us merely note that a major factor that prevents the sense of interaction between Legend Quest players simply may be lack of time. That is, if users were allowed to spend enough time "to get to know each other," they might develop a greater sense of awareness of being in a multiuser environment.[5] Other computer-graphics worlds, such as Morningstar and Farmer's two-dimensional Habitat (1991), in which users interact with each other for much longer (often several hours), can be seen as an example of such computer-mediated relations that have become more "sociable."

Since it is a game, Legend Quest may not be typical of other forms of VR, but it can highlight some important features of virtual worlds, such as some of the ways in which the experience of being inside such a world comes to be taken for granted. Conversely, other features have been identified that detract from this taken-for-grantedness, such as the sound of the user's footsteps or the awkwardness of the close bodily proximity in the virtual world of another user. One conclusion that emerges is that the user's experience of the environment, the ability to navigate within it, and the awareness of the other user are all determined not according to a single scale, such as "realism" or the fidelity of the input/output devices, but rather according to a complex set of factors that include the user's familiarity with other, similar technologies and devices.[6] If this conclusion seems a simple one, its significance can be underlined by noting that it goes against the grain of the conventional wisdom that the more "realistic" the environment and the input/output devices, the more absorbing the experience of the virtual world.[7]

To the abovementioned conclusion can be added that the experience of the virtual world will also be shaped by other, external factors, such as the length of use, the weight of the head-mounted display, and the physical space in which the user is able to move, that so far have not been elaborated. In the case of Legend Quest, the game features a relatively heavy (more than 2 kilograms) HMD, noticeable lag in the response of the virtual environment to the user, poor graphics resolution, and other features of a relatively low technical standard. These features are changing rapidly, however, so that the HMD on a more recent version of the game, for example, weighs only 600 grams, which is a relatively comfortable weight. Or again, the graphics of more recent games, although still cartoonlike, have become much more "realistic" thanks to the extensive use of texture-mapping—that is, providing textures on otherwise single-colored surfaces.

Walking vs. Flying Worlds

So much for the experience of the world of Legend Quest. How does it compare to experiences of other virtual worlds? We can begin by examining the modes of navigation. Most VR systems allow the user to navigate by means of a hand-held 3-D mouse. This is "cheating," of course, inasmuch as being inside a virtual world would ideally mean being able to walk or run in it. Sutherland's original "ultimate display," as noted earlier, made use of a mechanical device attached to the head to allow the user to look around in the virtual world—as opposed to walking or navigating by pointing—although what he was aiming at was a completely unencumbering device. Since then, a number of options for navigation have emerged.

As we have seen, in most VR systems, the user is physically confined within a small space, often limited by the available floor space or the length of the cable linking the HMD to the computer hardware. The user navigates by means of a hand-held 3-D mouse or points with a glove. The main alternatives here are optical or acoustic tracking systems (Meyer et al. 1992). Optical trackers work by means of calculating the distance between the user and the environment and can be divided into "outside in" systems, in which case the user wears the emitters and the sensors are fixed (for example, the user wears a head-mounted emitting device and there are cameras in the room picking up the signals), or "inside out" systems with mobile sensors and fixed emitters (the user wears head-mounted optical sensors that pick up signals from a set of emitters located around the room). Since the user can walk around in this world "freely," as in a real environment, we could call this a "walkabout" world.

With optical tracking users are free to use both hands. One example of a virtual world using an inside-out system is a VR system developed at the University of North Carolina. The content of the world is similar to that of others we have encountered: floating fish, busts on pillars, and other objects. The experience of being able to walk around within a confined space (of 10 by 12 feet), however, is quite different from the experience of other virtual worlds. The most striking aspects of this experience are the heaviness of the HMD, weighed down by the optical sensors, and the awkwardness of walking around dragging a heavy set of cables. This means that one has to be aware of where one is going in the real world for fear of tripping over the cables. It is difficult to see how the unnaturalness of the experience could be overcome, unless lightweight and unencumbering devices could be developed.

At the same time, there is an enhanced sense of presence in this kind of virtual world, especially because the gloved hand can be used to grope around or to manipulate objects rather than for navigation. The main advantage of walking without holding a device for navigation, then, is to be able to use one's hands. It is not clear, however, how significant the free use of the hands is, since, as was seen earlier, we are accustomed to using our hands for navigation. Hence the use of the hand and arm may not contribute very much to the sense of being absorbed in the virtual world, except in cases in which the focus in the virtual world is on manual tasks.

The main impression the user wearing optical trackers has of this virtual world is of being in a walkable space. As the virtual world in this case is room-sized, the user's inclination is to wander around the length and breadth of the room. But the measurements of the room the user is in can also be experienced as a constraint, because having the space of a room to walk in conveys the impression of being inside a cage.

Figure 5.2   Flying though a wall with a hand-held Fakespace BOOM.

The experience of flying provides a good contrast here, partly because it is the main alternative to walking in virtual worlds. Flying makes for a very different mode of experiencing the world. We can distinguish here between the experiences of flying at eye level or at bird's-eye level. One way that eye-level flying differs from walking is that it tends to be faster. The same applies to bird's-eye level flying, which simulates the ability to fly in the real world. Both types of flying experiences give the user the impression of being in control of a camera, since the user zooms around as if operating a movie camera or watching a film.

A concrete example of eye-level flying is the experience of moving across a landscape terrain created by the Fakespace BOOM, which in this case features push-button navigation on a hand-held counterbalanced stereoscopic viewing device (see Figures 5.2 and 5.3). The user has the illusion of moving across a landscape.

Figure 5.3   Landscape with buildings (from the same world as in Figure 5.2).

Again, because of our familiarity with driving an automobile and similar technologies, what the user experiences seems "natural." For reasons discussed earlier, the Fakespace BOOM allows a high-resolution display and practically lag-free tracking, so that the user's experience of flying around landscapes, which are rendered in great detail, is similar to the feeling of moving around in a real landscape—except faster.

The Fakespace BOOM also allows great agility, since it is possible to swivel around at sharp angles and to travel at great speeds. If moving through this realistic landscape seems akin to operating a camera or watching a film (motion pictures are often made with vehicle-mounted cameras), the difference is that in a film, the spectator does not control the narrative, whereas when flying around in a virtual landscape, the user controls the "camera" viewpoint.

In this sense, the experience is the opposite of the experience of walking in a constrained virtual space. The impression of flying freely is enhanced both by the content of the world, if, as in this case, the virtual world consists of a photo-realistic rendering of buildings, and by the device, which can be held or released at will. For these reasons, a suitable label for this world might be the "I am a camera" world. The trade-off is that one's hands are not available for any tasks apart from navigation (although it is possible to use the Fakespace BOOM with no hands, so that the user could, for example, operate a glove or a keyboard—see Figure 2.2).

The fact that flying around in a photo-realistic landscape does not necessarily entail a cameralike sensation can be illustrated by reference to the Fightertown cockpit simulator. This simulator game also features high-resolution texture-mapped graphics, and although it does not qualify as a VR experience, since it does not allow direct interaction with the virtual world (although there are affinities in terms of the technologies involved), it offers an instructive contrast.

Realistic flight-simulation yields an absorbing experience for two reasons: one is that the amount of concentration required for manipulating the flight controls dominates one's experience. The second is that simulated flying in a texture-mapped photo-realistic landscape, which includes objects, bodies of water, aircraft carriers, other planes, airports, and the like, is an experience that we are likely to be familiar with from games and films. This type of experience makes Fightertown an "action-adventure world," as opposed to one in which the user exercises bodily control over navigation.[8]

To pursue the comparisons between different modes of flying further, we can use another example—the Evans & Sutherland hang glider. Here, the user's body is suspended in the harness of a hang glider mock-up. As with a real hang glider, a crossbar controls the direction and altitude of the hang glider. The content of the virtual world, seen through a small aperture on a large-screen monitor, consists of a futuristic cityscape. This virtual world illustrates that flying can take different forms, because although hang glider flying requires a lot of concentration, the flying experience is much less demanding than in an aircraft simulator and therefore allows a more exploratory approach to flying. This simulation experience is as absorbing as that of aircraft simulation, but not in the manner of a fast-paced "action adventure." In short, there are different types of flying as well as differences between flying and walking in the virtual world, which, again, depend on the type of flying that we are used to in the real world, as well as on the content of the virtual world and on the devices used.

To underscore these differences in navigation, we can briefly point to some other features of simulator and computer games. Both types of games, like VR, typically involve a series of tasks. But in flight simulators, the experience is one of being in a vehicle, whereas in computer games like Sonic the Hedgehog or Streetfighter II, the user identifies with the screen character. These games may provide more absorbing experiences than watching television or than many VR experiences, but identification with an on-screen character or driving a vehicle is different from "being there" and flying or walking in the virtual world.

Moreover, the action is controlled in simulator and computer games by the narrative or the tasks that players are faced with, whereas in VR games, although some narrative is provided, the player typically has more control over the sequence of events. It is also possible to make another contrast: in simulator and computer games, players will fleetingly devote their attention to something else while the game is going on. When there is a break in the action or a pause between levels, for example, players may turn back to the real world. In VR games, by contrast, being immersed in the virtual world means that even such fleeting attention to the real world is impossible.

Working and Training Worlds

Apart from looking at content and the mode of navigating, another way to characterize the diversity of virtual worlds is by observing the uses to which they are put. Scientific visualization provides a good point of departure. Among the VR applications in this field are molecular visualization (Hann and Hubbard 1993), telesurgery and surgical training (Satava 1994), and the 3-D display of ultrasound images of patients' internal organs (Bajura et al. 1992). Even among these few examples of scientific visualization, there is a wide variety of experiences and devices. One device, for example, puts the scientist on the surface of an object at an atomic-scale level by using a scanning tunneling microscope (Taylor II et al. 1993). The surface is displayed in an HMD and the scientist can manipulate it with a force-feedback arm. In this virtual environment, although a sense of presence is created and interaction is possible, the "experience" is also one which, because of the content, is highly artificial. Manipulating an atomic-scale surface is not an experience that makes the user feel that he or she "is there," even if the experience of force in this case is useful for scientists in exploring and manipulating the structure of the surface. The same could be said for the experience of manipulating molecular models.

The experience of looking at the three-dimensional ultrasound image of a fetus in the same laboratory at the University of North Carolina, on the other hand, is one that feels disconcertingly "realistic," even if the display quality in this case is much lower than in the case of the atomic-scale surface and there is no interaction with the environment except for looking around the image with an HMD. This sense of "realism" has to do with the fact that a three-dimensional image of a real human being has associations for the user that are very different from those that come from visualizing atomic-level information.

It should be noted that this sense of "realism" is not only a question of the content of the virtual world, but also of the devices used: force-feedback provides a different experience of "presence" from merely visualizing an image with an HMD. And again, these two experiences differ in terms of "realism" and navigability from the "walk-about" and "I am a camera" worlds discussed previously—quite apart from the content of the respective virtual worlds.

"Realism" therefore depends not just on the content and the devices, but also on how VR compares with other everyday experiences. Unless we are used to working with robots, for example, the experience of force feedback will not be a familiar one. Watching animated films, however, fits into the repertoire of our experiences, so that a cartoonlike environment may create more of a sense of "presence" than a more realistically manipulable world. A different way to make this point is to recall the virtual worlds at the HITLab and at West Denton. The differences between the VR uses in these two classroom programs arose not only because desktop and immersive systems were used (since, apart from anything else, both sets of pupils built their worlds on desktop systems), but there were also differences because of the degree to which pupils became involved in creating their own virtual worlds. In other words, world-building, too, may make for a feeling of greater or lesser familiarity with the virtual world.[9]

To illustrate the variety of the kinds of "realism" in a different way, we can compare the educational applications of VR with VR uses in medical training. One feature of the HITLab and the West Denton projects was that pupils gained much from being able to learn how to build worlds cooperatively and being able to explore various ways of building worlds. This cooperation also allowed them to demonstrate their independence from teaching staff in various ways. The use of VR in medical training, by contrast, makes use of the fact that an experienced professional can provide guidance for the novice (Satava 1994:177–178).

Furthermore, whereas in the case of the HITLab and West Denton, the learning process depended to a large extent on the imaginativeness of virtual worlds, in medical training it is the "realism" or "true-to-lifeness" of the virtual training operation that counts. Not only are there different systems requirements in these cases, but the two types of systems also provide quite different experiences of virtual worlds.

It is easy to see that this variety of experiences of virtual worlds is compounded when we consider VR not as an information display technology, as we have done so far, but as a communications medium. For example, in the case of the multiuser game Legend Quest, one task that users jointly undertake consists of killing skeletons. But this task requires different skills and devices from, say, building a virtual world together or being tutored by someone in a virtual operation.

One of the implications of the variety of experiences of virtual worlds is that it is misleading to think of VR technology as developing in a single direction. VR as a technology is not simply on a trajectory toward a uniform type of realism, even if this is sometimes seen as the aim of researchers in the field of virtual reality. Instead, the nature of virtual worlds depends on the uses to which VR technology is put and the kinds of artifacts with which we are familiar—whether, for example, VR is used as a display device, communications medium, human-computer interface, or game; whether it is used at home or at work or as a means of telepresence; or again, what configuration of devices will be used.

These and other factors will determine how VR is experienced and regarded as part of our everyday lives. At the same time, there is no doubt that VR devices *have* developed in a single direction (and are likely to continue to do so) in the sense that the devices or tools for creating a sense of presence and allowing interaction have become more powerful. The variety of experiences of virtual worlds of VR can now be related back to the main argument of the book: I have suggested at several points in the course of this section that the experience of virtual worlds relates closely to what we are used to in our experience of the real world and with other technologies. If this is so, it might seem that our best guide for understanding VR would be experience with other technologies. This, however, would be to overlook the important point that although there may be similarities between experiences with one medium vs. another, there are also ways in which technologically-mediated experiences with VR share certain features that set them apart from other technologically-mediated experiences. The implications for the analysis of the relation between technology and social life is that it is only through an examination of the similarities and differences with other forms of everyday experience, technologically-mediated or not, that we can pinpoint the social implications of VR systems.

The Realities of Virtual Worlds[10]

To continue with our inventory of virtual worlds, we can now proceed somewhat differently. Thus far, we have investigated what kinds of experiences virtual worlds provide, both by comparison with each other and to some extent by comparison with other devices. At this point, we can ask a different question; namely, what are the most common or widespread virtual worlds? In other words, we can now turn our account of the range of virtual worlds inside out: instead of asking about the diversity of experiences inside computer-generated worlds, we can now ask, how common are these experiences? This account of how widespread different virtual worlds are will also allow us to compare the uses of virtual worlds with the uses of other technologies.

It will not be enough, however, to categorize the uses of VR in terms of isolated experiences. We shall also need to consider the contexts in which VR is being used, such as for entertainment, for education, or as an information display tool. Only taking into account the contexts will enable us to assess what inroads VR has actually made into the applications areas just mentioned. We shall also need to compare VR experiences with those of other technologies because, as we have seen, our experience with VR machines is shaped by our familiarity with other machines.

Two caveats are necessary before we start. First, the following list of common features is based on impressions rather than on data. This is the best those of us studying the field can do at this stage since, as far as I am aware, systematic information is not yet available. Second, the features listed apply only to existing VR systems. There is no suggestion that this list represents a reliable guide to the kinds of systems or experiences that can be expected in the future. The advantage of focusing on existing VR experiences, however, is that we will get a sense of some prevailing directions.

A final point before we proceed is that we shall need to present three lists of the most common features: the first with the most common features of VR experiences, the second with the most common technologies and their nearest technological equivalents, and the third with a combination of the two. Presenting the information this way will allow us gradually to put VR into a wider context.

Most Common Features of VR Experiences

1. Virtual worlds output is primarily visual. To those who are familiar with virtual reality technology, this may seem an obvious point. Nevertheless, it is a point worth stressing because VR is often seen as a technology that provides a complete virtual environment and allows interaction with all the senses. At present, most virtual environments are mainly visual, with sound output often limited to the sound of one or two objects in the virtual world or to voice-overs or music.

Sound is the second most common VR output capability, but even in the case of virtual worlds with elaborate aural output, what hearing adds to the experience of virtual worlds tends to make a limited impression on users. It needs to be noted immediately that lack of sound may not be as much of a restriction as one might think: Seeing a virtual environment provides a powerful sense of presence. Even though for example, we may not be able to smell a virtual world or feel the texture of objects, the lack of smell and texture pales to insignificance in comparison with the experience of seeing a virtual world.[11] We shall return to this concentration on vision, which we have already encountered in Heilig's attempt to attach different weightings to the senses, in the final chapter.

2. Input into virtual worlds mainly consists of point of view. Position-trackers, mostly on the user's head and hand, provide the typical means for the user's visual orientation in the environment. Even in cases in which users have a "virtual body" (with or without wearing a datasuit), it is not clear, as we have seen, how having a body enhances what can be *done* in a virtual world. It may, of course, enhance the sense of presence of the user, although this is an issue on which research has only begun. But what the user will be able to do with a body, of which there is typically only a visual representation, remains to be seen. Hence, too, the emphasis in VR has been placed

on changing point of view by moving forward not through real bodily movement but by doing the equivalent of pointing and clicking, whether with a glove or a hand-held 3-D mouse.

3. Interaction with virtual worlds mainly consists of changing the appearance of objects. The ability of users to manipulate the virtual world, if any, consists for the most part in being able to move objects, change their color, shoot things and the like.

4. Virtual worlds are most commonly operated by single users. Combining this with what has been said so far, this means that virtual worlds are mainly a means for an individual to look at a simulated world. Shared virtual worlds, which are much less common, are at present often no more than the equivalent of having a videophone conversation in a cartoon-style room.

5. The most common use of virtual worlds is for entertainment. Outside of the institutions engaged in research and development on VR systems, by far the largest number of VR systems, the largest number of users, and the largest amount of time have been devoted to shoot-'em-up and other games. "Walkthrough" models of kitchens or buildings and training environments are a distant second.

6. Experiences of virtual worlds tend to be short. This applies particularly to entertainment games, which typically last for a few minutes. The exceptions here are VR experiences related to research, which may be somewhat longer. Nevertheless, I am not aware of anyone who has spent a long time inside VR on a single occasion. Even if we consider the total amount of time spent by any one individual researcher or developer who frequently uses VR, it probably does not add up to a very long time, a few days perhaps.[12]

In the light of this list of features, we can immediately dismiss the exaggerated notion that VR will completely transform our sense of reality (a notion that we will encounter in the next chapter), as well as the notion that VR does not have any social implications. VR systems do not offer an alternative "reality"; they do, however, provide simulated worlds that seem "realistic," in certain respects, and they have specific implications in a number of contexts. Those who "hype" the technology and those who claim that it is "vaporware" are equally mistaken, inasmuch as they fail to recognize that VR has distinctive features, some of which are novel, in a limited range of settings. We can now follow up on this point by comparing VR to similar information and communication technologies (ICTs).

VR and Other Information and Communication Technologies

One general feature of new communication technologies, as Rogers has noted, is that they do not necessarily replace existing ones, but they transform them, as well as adding to and complementing them (1986:26). Thus VR may alter the landscape of existing ICTs, but it will often add to rather than supersede them. This is an important point to bear in mind while we set VR side by side with other ICTs. Since we have already listed some of the most common characteristics of VR, we can now proceed in the same order and identify which other ICTs share these characteristics in some measure.

1. As regards the visual emphasis of VR systems, the comparison must be with other computer games and other visual displays such as 3-D computer modeling. VR often represents an incremental advance here rather than a great leap in terms of the sophistication of content.

2. The input of point of view is perhaps the most distinctive feature of VR systems. This was already true of Sutherland's "ultimate display" system, despite the fact that he was aiming at something much greater—the "bullet that could kill you" in a virtual environment (1965:508). The nearest equivalent to present-day VR capabilities in terms of input of point of view are various types of simulators. This similarity is not surprising, inasmuch as the history of VR development, to some extent, intersects with that of simulators, whether they have been used for entertainment purposes, like Sensurround-type experiences, or for training, notably in flight simulations.

Yet the similarity between VR and simulators may be deceptive: The technical capabilities of VR may be close to those of simulators and simulators still often produce more powerful illusions of presence and interaction than VR systems. Yet simulators must nevertheless be regarded as "second person VR" (Heeter 1992:264); that is, the user is not experiencing the virtual environment directly, but from within a cockpit or similar constraint. By, so to speak, "freeing" the individual from the vehicle, which limits the scope of human perception and action, VR potentially makes a major difference to what can be done in the virtual environment, although, again, it may not do so in many current VR systems.

This last point needs to be seen in conjunction with the fact that, technically, great advances have been made in computer processing power (particularly in relation to 3-D graphics), position-tracking, and 3-D sound. From a technical point of view, the main requirement for achieving a higher degree of presence and interaction is even greater processing power. Once the process of refining existing systems is in place, these systems may not offer a "realistic" world, but they will offer very powerful visual—and, on a lesser scale of importance, aural—simulated or virtual environments.

3. The limited range of interaction in current VR systems suggests that its closest counterparts are existing visual tools for human-computer interaction (HCI).[13] But compared with conventional HCI tools, VR also allows users to navigate and explore the computer-generated environment.

4. The predominance of single-user VR systems can be put in context by noting that shared virtual worlds, at present, have the closest affinity with telecommunications devices such as the telephone, interactive television, videophones, and computer-mediated communication (CMC) like the Internet. The fact that VR systems are primarily for single users is an important limitation, since this puts them into the category of information rather than communication technologies (we shall return to this issue in Chapter 7).

In this context, however, it should also be mentioned that there has been a rapid expansion of CMC, and although most of it is currently text-based, the capacity to incorporate VR-like three-dimensional images within CMC has been demonstrated in a number of forms (such as the Virtual Reality Mark-up Language or VRML). Moreover, CMC is a medium in which users are absorbed for extensive periods; this applies not only to text-based but to image-based CMC, like Habitat.[14]

5. In relation to the point made above that the most popular use of VR systems is for entertainment games, there is little difference in terms of content between VR games and existing computer-based games. The main difference between VR games and other games appears to be that users are more cut off from the real world in VR. Whether players are also more involved or absorbed in VR games as opposed to other computer-based games, however, is not easily weighed, especially if the short duration of VR games is set against, say, the realism of VR graphics.

6. VR games might last much longer if they were to migrate from the arcade, where time is money, into the home. If they would also become as appealing as computer-based games or more so, they might also be used for much longer periods. At that point, the difference between VR games and existing computer games would become considerable: Although existing computer games are often played for

long periods, the social world nevertheless continues to circulate into and out of this kind of game playing.

With immersive VR games, and perhaps especially networked ones, this social aspect to playing games would no longer exist, given that VR games cannot be interrupted by the outside world in the same way conventional computer games can. But it is necessary to be careful here—both kinds of games can be interrupted, just not in the same way. It will only be possible to establish the difference by reference to actual patterns of use.

In relation to our attempt to pinpoint the unique contribution of VR to existing social contexts of technology, the most widespread impact of VR so far has been to enhance the sense of vividness of existing entertainment technologies. But perhaps the current appeal is mainly novelty rather than anything else. Apart from VR in the games context, the technology has taken its place beside other computer-based tools for scientific visualization and similar tasks. Together, the comparisons between VR and related ICTs suggest that VR systems make several distinctive, though still limited, differences to the ways we use existing ICTs. As VR is a relatively new technology, we would expect its effects to be limited, although the way VR has been portrayed in the media has implied that it is a much more "revolutionary" technology than it actually is (Biocca, Kim, and Levy 1995).

A Typology of Virtual Worlds and VR Experiences

Our inventories of the most common experiences of virtual worlds and of the closest experiences of similar technologies can now be combined. Before we link them, we can restate in a different way the justification for presenting the most common virtual worlds: one of the reasons why abstract typologies of VR such as those of Zeltzer (1992), Steuer (1995) and Robinett (1992) are unsatisfactory for examining the social implications of VR is that they represent ideal capabilities of VR systems that are still some way off. Talking about ideal capabilities may be useful for VR researchers, but it does not provide much help in examining the existing uses of VR. Only existing patterns of VR use can give an indication of their social implications. Bearing this in mind, we can now place these usage patterns alongside the uses of related technologies and experiences.

1. The most common content of virtual worlds consists of game fantasies (i.e., shooting spaceships), models of buildings (real or imaginary), training environments (landscapes, factories), models for

visualization (molecules, cadavers), and works of art (i.e., virtual galleries).[15] It should be admitted that this list is ambiguous, inasmuch as it conflates the number of types of virtual worlds that have been created with the number of times they have been used. But perhaps the number of worlds created and the number of users generally overlap. VR demonstrations at exhibitions and in labs have also been among the most common uses of VR, but they should be counted as prototypes rather than as everyday uses. The use of VR for demonstrations and games also explains the brevity of VR experiences.

One question that can be raised here is whether the content of virtual worlds tends in each case to represent more "realistic" or imaginary worlds. The balance, so far, has been toward the latter. Importing recorded visual material into virtual environments may, however, alter the balance toward more realism in the content of virtual worlds. This realistic content can be incorporated into virtual worlds by means of shape acquisition technologies, although they are still rare (Biocca and Delaney 1995:111–113). The fact that designing objects is the most labor-intensive programming task in VR may, however, make these devices appealing to VR developers (the same devices are, of course, also being used and developed by computer games manufacturers and film studios).

2. The most common realms of application are entertainment, training (including education), and visualization (architecture, medicine). We could add the category of VR as a tool for telepresence or as a communications medium, since there are a number of networked VR systems. At present, however, VR in this sense is still confined to a handful of pilot projects such as SIMNET and VIRTUOSI. If we were to add networked VR here, the question would become whether the category of communication tools should remain separate, or if it should be subsumed under the other realms of application.

3. The most widespread devices are HMDs and 3-D flying mice (or joysticks). Gloves, datasuits, and spaceballs are becoming rare. The most common form of input is therefore from the head and the hand or arm. Input from the rest of the body is less common. The most popular mode of navigation is to change the point of view by moving the head and pushing a button to walk or fly. Full-body motion with input from the real body, again, has become exceptional.

One feature that deserves highlighting is that in the vast majority of existing VR systems, a hand is required for navigation. The exceptions are datasuits or treadmills, which allow walking, but both are uncommon. And although some systems allow users physically to roam around (in a space the size of a small room, for example, with the use of optical trackers or in CAVE-type systems), again such systems are rare compared with the majority of systems, which confine users to a space within a few feet of where they are standing or sitting. Apart from these popular configurations, there are, of course, a number of other input and output options, such as speech recognition and force-feedback.

At this point, instead of continuing our comparison in relation to points 4, 5, and 6 (we have already done so to a large extent in the previous section), we can now pursue a broader issue: the sense of "presence" and "interaction"—or combining the two, of "immersion"—in VR compared with other ICTs. Before making the comparison, it needs to be mentioned that desktop VR is far less "immersive" than systems with an HMD and hand/arm input. Hence, we shall restrict ourselves to the latter, even though, as we have seen, there is a considerable range within the category of desktop systems, and the boundaries are blurred since desktop virtual worlds can be transferred onto immersive systems (and vice versa).

In the light of the features we have identified in this section, VR can be considered more immersive than other professional visualization tools such as 3-D desktop CAD tools or 2-D representations on computer screens, since the latter do not allow the same kind of direct interaction with the display. VR also offers a more direct sense of involvement than training simulators, although whether this entails that VR is more absorbing or engaging, again, depends, among other things, on the "realism" of the simulator environment.

As for entertainment, VR is a more immersive experience than watching television, but it is similar to existing simulator entertainment experiences. As a tool for communication, finally, videophones probably offer a stronger sense of "immersion" than shared VR, but perhaps that may be a result of users' limited experience with networked VR technology and of the short period of time that users typically spend inside shared virtual worlds. On the other hand, VR is more immersive than text-based CMC like multiuser dungeons games, although, again, these are perhaps intellectually or emotionally more engrossing (Bruckmann and Resnick 1995; Bartle 1990).

Several comments are needed in relation to what has just been said. The first is to stress again that the conclusions I have presented in this section are based on impressions rather than on data. It may be possible one day to measure "presence and interaction" or "immersion" in a scientific way. Even so, the degree of immersion is bound to vary according to users, devices, and content. Nevertheless, it seems useful to have made an attempt at a straightforward comparison because it allows us to get a sense of the relation between VR and other technologies.[16]

One additional dimension that might be useful is the extent to which the user is aware of other users in the case of shared virtual worlds (see Benford and Fahlén 1992). Instead of complicating the comparisons that have just been made, it can suffice here to add that if we follow what has been said so far, the user in shared VR systems is more aware of other users than in (text-based) CMC and in multiplayer computer games, but less so than, say, in videophones.

Multiparticipant simulators are difficult to compare, as are the various shared VR uses for professional visualization and training, since the ability to cooperate with other users in these systems is highly dependent on the tasks involved. Nevertheless, it can be ventured that these shared work-related VR environments allow joint spatial tasks to be carried out more effectively than in similar technologies.

These comparisons suggest that VR development and VR uses do not consist of a single pattern. One point that follows from this (which, again, sits uneasily with those who overestimate or underestimate the implications of VR) is that the need for different types of VR in different applications realms is pushing toward a range of systems, from the sophisticated and high-powered to the relatively low-powered and rudimentary. Even if the most common form of VR, entertainment games, is often indistinguishable from existing computer games or simulators, VR nevertheless consists of a range of devices that offer tools and experiences that differ from other technologies.

In light of what has been said about the nature and the various uses of VR systems, we can now venture some generalizations about VR and its relation to other technologies. First, there are few indications, apart from the experience with prototype systems, of how shared worlds may compare with the worlds of existing communication tools. The link with other communication technologies, when it is made, will nevertheless be focused on the fact that VR input mainly consists of point of view and that navigation in the virtual world differs from conventional ways of using ICTs.[17] Still, at the moment, VR is mainly a stand-alone technology; the most widespread use comes from single-user systems.

Second, the relation between VR and other professional visualization tools hinges on the possibility that VR may supersede existing devices in terms of functionality—in other words, whether the mode of visualization by means of VR has a better "fit" with the requirements of the user and the task.

Our use of VR—and especially the combination of visual output and navigational input—thus maps closely onto our existing uses of ICTs. Or, to put it the other way around, the fact that VR relies so much on visual output and manual navigation has not been because the development of devices for the other senses has been lacking. Heilig's (1992) multisensory cinema was, after all, first described in 1953 and implemented not long thereafter, and tactile computer-generated display devices were demonstrated approximately two decades later (Noll 1972). Nevertheless, the output of VR is mainly visual, and the "user-friendliness" of VR depends to a large extent on the ease of navigation. The key aspects of VR that have been listed here—rather than the various capabilities that have been attributed to future VR systems—are therefore competing with and adding to existing technologies.

In the final chapter, we shall need to place this inventory of VR experiences into the larger context of the institutions that are pursuing research and development, on the one hand, and the pressures for the emergence of certain types of applications, on the other. As we have seen, VR systems are in fact developing in at least two directions that are dependent on a number of factors, including commercial success, the competition and compatibility of VR with existing devices and how we use them, and the achievements and constraints within VR research and development. VR has several dominant forms, and the differences among them mean that VR systems are supplanting other devices or technologies in certain areas—and are becoming integrated with or complementing the other devices or technologies in other areas. It has been claimed that virtual reality allows us to create worlds that were hitherto beyond the bounds of our imagination (Lanier 1989:8; Laurel 1991:198). But if the content of existing virtual worlds is anything to go by, it seems that VR has much in common with conventional uses of ICTs—even if VR technology transforms and adds to these uses in distinctive ways.

6

The Spirit in the Machine

In recent years, computer-related technologies, including virtual reality, the Internet, and artificial intelligence, have given rise to new ways of thinking about the role of technology in society. This new mode of thought can be labeled cyberculture, and central to it is the notion that new technologies can radically alter the way we live. Here we shall examine cyberculture mainly in relation to VR, as these ideas are bound to shape the image of VR technology, much as the ideas of "hackers" shaped the image of the personal computer. But cyberculture is also part of a wider shift in our conception of technology and I shall argue that even if the cybercultural worldview is closer to science fiction than to the current state of science and technology, it is nevertheless worth examining, since this wider shift may have far-reaching implications.

Cyberculture has a number of incarnations, including academic theorizing and youth culture. What they have in common is a vision of the future in which technology radically alters the relation between humans and machines and thus gives rise to new cultural possibilities. Some of the pioneers of VR technology, including Brenda Laurel and Jaron Lanier, have been among the principal exponents of cybercultural ideas, suggesting that the creation of virtual worlds and of shared cyberspaces will have revolutionary social consequences and allow hitherto unimagined forms of human expression.

Laurel and Lanier's view is echoed in the work of academic theorists like Donna Haraway and Alluquere Rosanne Stone, who believe that new technologies may have radical political ramifications, an idea they pursue through the image of cyborgs that blur the distinction between humans and machines.[1] Within youth culture, these themes find expression, for example, in magazines such as *Wired* and in cyberpunk nightclubs and cafes in London and San Francisco. Here again, we find an agenda for cultural and political change premised on innovations in computing and other technologies.

Surfing the Soul[2]

Before we can locate the cybercultural worldview within the larger context of current thinking about technology, we need to examine some of its manifestations. The first place we can look is among those who have been involved in developing VR technology itself. The most well-known visionaries in this group are Brenda Laurel and Jaron Lanier, both promoters of the technology when it first began to attract widespread attention and still involved in the VR industry.[3]

Prophetic notions abound in their public utterances. Thus Lanier speaks of "an experience when you are dreaming of all possibilities being there, that anything can happen, and it is just an open world where your mind is the only limitation . . . The thing that I think is so exciting about virtual reality is that . . . it gives us this sense of being able to be who we are without limitation; for our imagination to become shared with other people" (1989:8). Nevertheless, he cautions that "there is a really serious danger of expectations being raised too high."[4]

With Laurel we find a similar juxtaposition of other-worldliness and realism. "With virtual reality systems," she writes, "the future is quite literally within our grasp" (1991:197). It will "blow a hole in all our old imaginings and expectations. Through that hole we can glimpse a world of which both cause and effect are a quantum leap in human evolution" (1991:198), a suggestive image even if it is not quite clear what the second part of the sentence means. In a somewhat different vein, she writes: "I think that we can someday have Dionysian experiences in virtual reality, and that they will be experiences of the most intimate and powerful kind . . . Dionysian experience is the experience of being *in the living presence* of not only the artist but also huge spiritual forces" (1991:196). Although she also cautions: "It seems that there are some rather serious obstacles to be overcome before virtual reality can deliver the robust kinds of experiences that we fantasize about" (1991:186).

An extension of this vision is that Laurel thinks that there will be some kind of merging between VR machines and humans. She refers to these human-machines as "fusion people."[5] This is one of the many points where there are direct continuities between the prophetic developers of VR and academic writing on cyberculture, and we may therefore pursue the cybercultural worldview further in these writings.

Academic theorists derive their inspiration not so much from VR systems as such, but from this human-machine fusion.[6] Alongside a far-reaching vision based on the possibilities of the new technology, there is a political and cultural program. Metaphors abound in these accounts of the future. In Stone's "evocation of cyberspace," we find her describing the "cybernetic act" as consisting of "the desire to cross the human/machine boundary . . . a desire literally to enter into such a discourse, to penetrate the smooth and relatively affectless surface of the electronic screen and enter the deep, complex, and tactile (individual) cybernetic space or the (consensual) cyberspace within and beyond" (1991:108–109). But again, there are some thisworldly obstacles to these otherworldly pleasures: "No refigured virtual body, no matter how beautiful, will slow the death of a cyberpunk with AIDS" (1991:113).

Bodily cyberpursuits are thus part of the political agenda of cyberculture. Another aspect is gender politics. Haraway "would rather be a cyborg than a goddess" (1991:181). Her idea of doing away with the "troubling dualisms" (1991:177) within the Western tradition and thus realizing a "utopian dream of the hope for a monstrous world without gender" rests on "high-tech culture [which] challenges these dualisms in intriguing ways" (1991:177), including, for example, that "cyborgs might consider more seriously the partial, fluid, sometimes aspect of sex and sexual embodiment" (1991:180). In her "cyborg manifesto . . . liberation rests on the construction of the consciousness . . . of possibility . . . this is a struggle over life and death, but the boundary between science fiction and social reality is an optical illusion" (1991:149). Hence, her cyborg is "not utopian nor imaginary; s/he is virtual" (1992:329).

Cybercultural ideas have been particularly influential in cultural studies, in the study of science and technology, and in anthropology. For example, "cyborg anthropology" was the name of one of the panels at the 1992 annual meeting of the American Anthropological Association (see also Escobar 1994). One common feature of these new ideas in the fields just mentioned is the notion that advances in computer technology will provide the vehicle for new ways of life. The same premise also forms the basis for the atmosphere currently generated in cyberpunk nightclubs and cafes. If the "liberation" to which Haraway refers seems to take place at the level of theoretical debate in scholarly books and journals, a similar change in consciousness and lifestyle seems to be emerging within certain strands of youth culture.

At the Cyberseed Club in London, for example, the compere, Brian Davis, announcing the evening's program, enjoins the audience to "surf the soul" and to "mellow out."[7] Identifying himself and the audience as cyberpunks, the content of his brief introductory talk is designed to put his listeners in the right mood for the evening's entertainment. He proclaims that "science is magic" and goes on to explain how the frame of mind of clubgoers should be informed by this insight. In a similar vein, Martin Kavanagh, leader of the United Kingdom's VR User's Group, outlines the group's activities and announces the activities of the "Virtualitea" (sic) room of the club where the computers are located.

The Cyberseed program itself consists of a live performance of Japanese new-age music, as well as the club's regular recorded "rave" music. The promotional leaflet promises "altered images, altered sounds, altered minds, and altered states" and lists among the club's attractions "VR machines, Sega computer games, psychoactive cocktails, brain machines, cyber and VR demos, massage, tarot, and guest cyberscientists and artists."

These attractions take place in three dark and interconnected cellar rooms, two of which contain bars. In the largest of these rooms, various graphic and photographic images are projected onto the walls, including colorful contemporary works of art and pictures of faraway places and peoples. These images change frequently and since they envelop the room, they could be said to give the impression of a VR-like experience. The second room features a bar with "psychoactive cocktails" (drinks containing "smart drugs") and is otherwise given over to massage and tarot. It is the third room, however, that features the computing element of the club. There the clientele is gathered around three personal computers, one displaying fractal images, a second operating a computer game, and a third called the "brain machine." This machine consists of a computer-synchronized stroboscopic light operated via head-mounted glasses and earphones. The user who wears these, according to the accompanying leaflet, "can experience deep relaxation, concentration/accelerated learning; a new sense of the body; hallucinations and great visuals, [and] true alterations of consciousness."

By midnight, attendance has reached between thirty and forty young people who pursue the computer-related activities, dance, or sit in a meditative state during the new-age music performance and talks. Although the audience is similar to that at other clubs in London, the atmosphere in the Cyberseed Club is unique insofar as the activities are more subdued or "mellow." Rather than focusing exclusively on dancing, clubgoers wander around among the various attractions, seeking, it seems, to "alter" their mood or consciousness.

But although the club announces itself as "Europe's First Virtual Reality Club," the connection with the technology itself is tangential. The way computers are used may be unusual for a nightclub; however, the main connection to actual VR systems is the commercial Virtuality VR games machine (£1 or $1.50 per minute of play) at the entrance of the club, which is available "at a reduced price," as the compere points out, for clubgoers.

At the Horseshoe Cafe in San Francisco, the connection with VR is more remote still, despite the fact that references to VR feature prominently.[8] On a shelf next to the bar is an array of leaflets announcing forthcoming club attractions, including "mind-melting visuals" in the "Virtual Reality" club, "look/see projections and hyperdelic video" at the "Carefree" event, and "live interactive adventures" and "media immersion" at the "12 Hour mysterious Salad." The music announced for these events is similar to that playing in the background at the Horseshoe Cafe itself.

The main connection with VR at the cafe, however, is a personal computer in an alcove toward the back of the establishment. The screen of this personal computer is built horizontally into a table with the keyboard on one side. Several people, dressed mostly in black with T-shirts featuring science fiction logos, are crowded around the table, their attention absorbed by the computer screen which is part of SF (San Francisco) NET, an electronic mail network (or "bulletin board") that provides a forum for discussion among eighteen locales in the San Francisco area (at fifty cents for twenty minutes). The Horseshoe Cafe is one of the focal points of this network, with other participating cafes and locations listed in a leaflet next to the computer. It also lists a variety of discussion topics, including "politics, environment, astrology, science/technology, [and] philosophy." The leaflet announces that "the information age is upon us and it is not just a sterile world of numbers and statistics. It is also a world of people and the amount of information each person represents."

The discussions on this information exchange network are explicitly identified with cyberculture both by users and by the club owner, Wayne Gregori. Gregori refers to those who send abusive messages as "cyberjerks," whereas another user or "netsurfer," whose network name is "*Cyber Monk*," refers to his "cyberfamily" (quoted in Bishop 1992:21). Apart from the difference in VR-related equipment between the two venues, there is also a different atmosphere at the Horseshoe Cafe. The cafe occupies a large room with a large shopfront window that faces the street and it is open not only during nightclub hours but also during conventional restaurant business hours.

Among the forty or so customers, the beverage of choice is coffee, again of the more conventionally psychoactive type, but served in the large variety that is customary in the San Francisco area. The main activity—apart from conversation—consists of reading the newspapers and books that are lying scattered among the tables. Science fiction seems to be the favored genre, although Lewis Mumford and Jean Baudrillard were also in evidence. Despite the similarities between the young and fashionably dressed participants in both the London club and the San Francisco cafe, the Horseshoe Cafe mainly offers an atmosphere of relaxed conversation, whether electronically or in the more traditional cafe style.

Again, although the connection with VR technology itself is limited, the Horseshoe Cafe clearly partakes of cyberculture inasmuch as the prefix "cyber" is used to designate "immaterial" forms of communication via electronic media.[9] This sense of the term, which also evokes a vision of the future in which VR-like technologies abound, provides the theme around which the Horseshoe Cafe is based. Compared with the Cyberseed Club, which promotes altered consciousness through arts-related activity, the Horseshoe Cafe seems to be more oriented to consciousness-alteration by means of "bookish" pursuits—but perhaps this is a difference in style rather than substance. If both clubs are drawing on the publicity surrounding VR technology, their main connection with it lies in fostering the "consciousness" attendant upon its future uses.

Even if technological innovations have on other occasions generated new cultural trends, the link between the developers of the technology, academic theorists, and youth culture in this case seems to be particularly intimate. Laurel, for example, acknowledges Stone's work as an important influence,[10] whereas Haraway thinks that the work of "story-tellers exploring . . . high-tech worlds" ought to "inform late twentieth-century political imaginations."[11]

Or again, the politics of information and of gender of the United Kingdom Virtual Reality User's Group Newsletter, which partly provides the inspiration of the Cyberseed Club, bear a strong resemblance to the politics of the academic theorists and the visionary developers of the technology. Elsewhere, cyberpunks have been described as the "shock troops of postmodernism" (McCaffery 1991:back cover). Meanwhile, Lanier's and Laurel's ideas about consciousness alteration are closely in keeping with the themes of both VR-related venues—as, incidentally, are their styles of dress. These affinities and reciprocal influences among theorists, VR developers, and youth culture could be added to at length. They all point to a common worldview and a common way of life among the members of a cultural avant-garde in London and on the west coast of the United States, two global centers of the information and communication technology industries.

New Romancers[12]

Cybercultural phenomena first appeared around the same time as the VR take-off. They have since become more commonplace, with the proliferation, for example, of VR-themed cafés and cafés with Internet connections. But these phenomena need to be put into a larger context. At first sight, the incorporation of new technological developments within the worldview of culture carriers seems to be ill-suited to a period in which there is widespread scepticism about scientific and technological achievements. Yet as we shall see, cyberculture is part of a more fundamental reinterpretation of the importance of science and technology which, when it is placed in the social context of its carriers, not only fits well with this scepticism but is likely to endure. This appeal of cyberculture can best be explored by reference to Weber's disenchantment thesis.

More than seventy-five years ago, in the lecture "Science as a Vocation," Weber talked of the "disenchantment of the world" (1948: 155; first published in 1919) by science, by which he meant that science had replaced meaningful worldviews with impersonal explanations of the world and of nature. Nevertheless, he recognized that intellectual strata would remain predisposed toward endowing the world with meaning. Thus he spoke of "the need of some modern intellectuals to furnish their souls with . . . guaranteed genuine antiques . . . by way of [a] substitute [for religion] . . . they produce surrogates through all sorts of psychic experiences to which they ascribe the dignity of mystic holiness" (1948:154).

But what if these substitutes for religion are no longer available? What if, instead, certain advances within science and technology themselves come to be seen as the key to producing new forms of expression or new psychic experiences? These notions of the transcendence of the mundane uses of technology lie at the heart of cyberculture.

One common feature of the ideas and practices outlined above is that future ICTs will make possible radically new forms of human self-expression and that these, in turn, will herald a new technology-centered era that will release human beings from the material constraints of their current lives. Since the dehumanizing effects of science and technology are, paradoxically, among these, the cybercultural worldview envisions a fusion of science and art, with the former providing the means and the latter the cultural ends. Eventually, with the emergence of a society in which communication in cyberspace becomes all-important, the pioneering carriers of this worldview may create a completely new culture.

There is, however, a central tension within this worldview. On the one hand, its future promise relies on technological innovation, on purely technical or instrumental advances within specialist fields of research and the production of machinery. On the other hand, real advancement of this vision of the future can only come about through cultural innovation, through new patterns of thinking and of experience—and these alone.

This tension stems partly from the high premium placed on the sphere of culture. The fascination with ICTs typically derives from the fact that they offer a seemingly endless supply of novel experiences, the consumption of which plays an ever greater role within advanced societies, particularly in the home.[13] VR systems seem to provide the perfect extension of this trend, since they hold out the promise that human beings may one day be able to live within computer-generated virtual worlds limited only by their imaginations. If such a way of life should come about, it would represent, in Weberian terms, a completely reenchanted world.

At the same time, from a purely technical viewpoint, as we have seen, the aim toward which the development of VR systems is advancing is to establish how the senses operate, on the one hand, and to provide machine-generated environments that can be manipulated, on the other. If VR machines could provide an impersonally manufactured and calculated stimulation of the senses, then far from providing a limitless sensorium of the imagination and reenchanting the world, as the cybercultural worldview would have it, they might become a means of disenchanting what was previously one of the last refuges from the disenchantment of the world, namely human perception and experience. Science and technology in this case would not only dominate the external world, but could offer a machine-generated environment for the awareness that human beings have of the world—albeit an artificial one.

These possible consequences of VR technology are not spelled out here in order to set a technocratic dystopia against the utopian elements of the cybercultural worldview. After all, how VR systems are developed and the uses to which they are put are not subject to scientific and technical aims alone. The point is to contrast the problems that need to be solved in VR by scientific and technological means with the worldview to which this technology has given rise, which consists of projecting onto the technology various human wishes for fulfilment. This tension, between mundane technical problem-solving and extra-mundane visions of the future, or, to employ Weber's terms again, between instrumental rationality and value-rationality, is one that we can expect to continue reproducing itself throughout the various manifestations of cyberculture.

Having given a brief account of some of the ideas and activities of these three closely related groups of culture-carriers, the cybercultural worldview can now be located in a wider social and cultural context which, I shall argue, provides fertile soil for its continued appeal. The material basis of this worldview is the growing economic importance of ICTs in advanced societies. This aspect of contemporary social life is well documented. Information and communication technologies now occupy a central place in the economies of advanced societies (Beniger 1986). To this must be added the continuous expansion of institutions of higher learning, which provides an enlarged base for the employment of commentators on the cultural industries and their products (Collins 1992:92–94). These two growth areas overlap and reinforce each other, with the rising demand for expertise in the mass media and information technologies contributing to the growing market for the products of cultural industries and vice versa.

Equally powerful perhaps is the ideal basis of this worldview. Cyberculture derives its strength from a major current within contemporary intellectual life that tends toward a romanticization of culture and of science through a merger between the two. The idea that culture and science will become thoroughly intertwined can be seen as a product of the growing autonomy of academic ideas from social life, so that the mundane role of science and technology in providing the engine of economic growth can be ignored, whereas the merged realm of science/culture is invested with a life of its own.

The theoretical ground for this cybercultural fusion of science and art has been prepared for some time, especially among philosophers and sociologists of science. So, for example, Feyerabend denies the efficacy of science and invokes Dadaism as an alternative scientific method (Feyerabend 1978:100–105, 120). Similarly, within the sociology of science, the focus has recently come to be placed on the representational and literary qualities of scientific knowledge, rather than on its instrumental or wealth-creating consequences (for example, Woolgar 1988).

The fascination with science as a form of culture within cyborg postmodernism is, incidentally, perfectly compatible with a viewpoint that rejects science, insofar as once science has become subsumed within sociocultural life or merged with art, its effects need no longer be seen as the feared "external" ones of an instrumental domination of nature or society.

The version of overcoming the tension within this worldview within youth culture is slightly different from the academic one. Here, the idea is to emphasize the countercultural possibilities of technology. Thus cyberculturalists see themselves as outlaws or renegades. As Elmer-Dewitt puts it, they have "a way of looking at the world that combines an infatuation with high-tech tools [with] a disdain for conventional ways of using them" (1993:59).

Although cyberculture is mainly sustained by the social organization of intellectual life, it is also a product of advances in computing and related technologies. VR is well placed to occupy a central place among these advances since, as we have seen, resources are being devoted to the development of VR and related technologies on an increasing scale. As long as innovation continues within VR and related technology, cyberculture will continue to be able to draw on the promise that future innovations may bring, thus sustaining its dream of a merger between science and art and of finding new outlets for self-expression in the creation of new worlds by means of advanced ICTs.

The wider context for this appeal is the shift in thinking about science and the expectation of deriving meaning from science. Such hopes that science may herald the dawn of a new age are not new. They also accompanied the advent of the "steam age" and the "space age," for example. Yet since VR technology, like the Internet, seemingly creates a whole new horizon for human expression, and since science is no longer seen as a tool for mastery over the world, but rather as the handmaiden of magic, perhaps VR is a perfect vehicle for the belief in merging human beings with information and communication machines, or the belief that cyborgs represent a form of consciousness suited to the new age.

Whatever the case may be in VR research and industry, cyberculture is likely to continue to provide an inspirational view of science and technology within contemporary culture. The reality of cyberculture, however, will remain the Weberian one whereby beliefs reflect the predispositions of the intellectual strata which are their carriers, as well as the Durkheimian one whereby the role of knowledge and belief mirrors more fundamental features of social reality.[14]

Whether, in addition, we can discover the "cyborgs in us all" (Downey 1992:3) or experience hitherto unimagined states of consciousness within our computer-simulated environments remains to be seen. But the conditions that have thus far sustained cybercultural ideals, whether technological, social, or cultural, are likely to be with us for some time yet.[15]

So far, we have examined how technologies such as VR have given rise to a new cultural movement. Yet cyberculture is mainly the preserve of intellectual strata, of a small number of gurus who have seized on the futuristic and expressivist possibilities of the technology and promise personal salvation to a select following within youth culture. These gurus may have played a key role in presenting VR to the public, but VR has also had a widespread popular appeal apart from youth culture. During the take-off years, VR received a great deal of publicity in the mass media. This often took the form of dwelling on the more sensationalist and futuristic possibilities of VR, such as virtual sex, addiction to VR, and the like. A few examples can be given here to show that whereas the ideas of intellectual strata remain in tension with the mundane uses of technology, within popular culture, new technology and the uncertainties that it supposedly brings must be reembedded in everyday life.[16]

In early 1994, the magazine of the Jehovah's Witnesses sect, *The Plain Truth,* devoted a cover story to VR, "Virtual Reality—Creating Your Own Values?" (Halford 1994). The cover illustration shows a hand wearing a glove with a computer screen motif reaching to pick an apple, presumably an allusion to the tree of knowledge. After a competent account of some of the available VR systems, which stresses the new possibilities offered by the technology, the essay turns to the "sinister side" of VR. The article mentions "virtual sex" and "virtual sadism" among the "virtual sins" (1994:18), but adds: "VR goes beyond any medium thus far developed. It leaves a *real* impact and this illusion of reality can be extremely addictive" (1994:19). In keeping with the view that what matters is not the technology but how it is used, the article cautions: "VR is not, of itself, sinful. But if people have an appetite for what God's law has placed off limits, VR will provide unprecedented opportunities to indulge in it. If (or rather when) VR becomes accessible, we will need to use it selectively" (1994:19).

We have already seen that VR may lead to moral panics. But it can also be regarded as beneficial: "Christians will almost certainly try to harness the power of VR, just as they now use the computer, as an aid to Bible study and for other educational and inspirational purposes . . . But we must be careful. Remember, this is a technology that enables the user to decide what is real . . . VR offers the ultimate in escapism" (1994:19). Religious belief cannot simply rule out the use of new technologies, it can only encourage caution: "If . . . as has been suggested, VR gives us the power to decide what we shall be, we shall need to be extremely careful how we use it" (1994:19).

Another theme is the distortion of reality by VR technology, which is put into a religious perspective: "God does not 'airlift' you out of problems . . . He guides and supports you through a lifetime of experiences—*real* experiences that are the anvil upon which *real* faith is forged" (1994:19). Accounts of VR in the mass media typically state that the technology is bound to have both good and bad effects and that it remains to be seen which will prevail. From a religious viewpoint, however, this idea must be embedded in the notion that there is a more firm reality on which believers can rely.

This article can be compared with an article in the journal *The Marxist*. Its feature on "Video Games and Virtual Reality" made the point that VR games "will inhibit independence of thought" and have a "mind-deadening effect, by putting humanity—or at least those who can afford it—in thrall to a machine . . . There will come a time when fewer and fewer young people . . . feel the need to experience the world at first hand" (1994:24). The reality is that "capitalism . . . creates the demand and . . . sees large profit in peddling these over-priced, ever smarter computer devices that nobody really needs" (1994:21). VR thus reaffirms faith in the more fundamental realities elaborated by Marx.

It is also important that "revolutionary" technology does not disrupt faith in institutions. A good illustration is provided by an advertisement for a new high-tech format for the presentation of the British Broadcasting Corporation (BBC) television news. The technology in this case included what was described as VR. In fact, it consisted of two innovations that were not VR: an introductory sequence with a computer-generated 3–D "glass" logo of the BBC in which "the glass appears to refract and reflect light naturally, but . . . does not really exist" (Fox 1993:22), and a "virtual newsroom," a computer-generated newsroom in which "even the studio floor will not actually exist. Only the newsreaders will be real" (Watts and Leapman 1993:6). In other words, here, as elsewhere, VR technology is referred to as any computer graphics technology that creates simulated environments.

Nevertheless, the BBC initiative was described as "a high-tech leap . . . into a brave news world of 'virtual reality'" (Watts and Leapman 1994:6). The article went on: "One ill-timed software glitch, and the whole image could disintegrate. But if virtual reality goes wrong in the middle of a program, real reality will take over" in the form of the old studio set (Watts and Leapman 1994:6).

What is interesting here is that this radical departure had to be integrated with the traditional image of the BBC as a reliable and trustworthy institution. The advertising campaign accompanying the "new look" of the program (featuring a picture of the new logo) declared that the BBC has a "reputation for accuracy and integrity that is recognized the world over. And whatever else may change, as technology advances and design styles evolve, those essential qualities will remain constant."[17] In other words, like the god of Jehovah's Witnesses or Marxist insights into the opiates of the masses, the BBC's enduring reputation provides a deeper or more permanent reality that can be relied upon even during periods of technological transformation. And although intellectuals may wish to surf on the crest of this transformation, popular culture generally prefers to view it from safer shores.

7

Virtual Worlds and the Social Realities of Technology

Virtual reality technology is still at an early stage of development. Yet within a short time, VR systems have gone from Lanier's unwieldy prototype to a variety of devices used in everyday settings, including products aimed at the consumer market. This book has examined the genesis of this technology and a number of contexts in which it is used. One of its central arguments has been that, to get a sense of the social implications of new technologies, technological and social change must be examined conjointly at several interrelated levels. It now remains for us to draw these levels together and to return to the significance of this study for the understanding of new technologies.

First then, to connect these levels, it may be useful to give a brief summary of the career of VR technology. VR systems have congealed into several types of devices with a specific range of capabilities. This does not mean that the shape of this set of artifacts will remain on a predetermined track: advances in research, new design options, as well as the contexts of application will all continue to shift VR in different directions.

But from the vantage point of the sociology of technology, certain tracks of VR development have already become more pronounced than others. This pattern, whereby the technology has become refined in certain ways, allowing for certain types of manipulation of the world, cannot be explained by reference to "social shaping" or to the economic "pull" of markets alone. Instead, a number of scientific and technological advances, such as the increasing speed of computer graphics processing and enhanced position-tracking accuracy, have facilitated improvements in VR technology. These advances, however,

137

do not determine the specific devices that have been produced or those that have found their way to commercial success. Artifacts have their own trajectories, but they also congeal around the fit between their capabilities and the uses to which they are put.

We can now fill in this overall dynamic with the details of VR development. Between the late 1950s and the mid-1980s, computer technology advanced rapidly and there was a fundamental change in the function of computers. Initially, the computer was a calculating machine, but by the end of that period, it had become, among other things, a tool for writing, for communication, for visualization, and for entertainment. Sutherland's "ultimate display" was to be an interface to the computer, a means of accessing and manipulating data. This idea remains influential, but the function of VR, too, has been broadened by the transformation in computing. VR systems are no longer merely a means for human-computer interaction but also a tool for visualization, gaming, training, communication, and other applications.

The changing function of computers and the increase in processing power both contributed to the emergence of VR. Yet VR systems only took off in the early 1990s after Lanier's demonstration of a commercial VR system that had an appeal beyond the scientific and military communities. Since then, a number of university-based institutions have established their place on a steadily advancing VR research front, and dozens of firms have begun to produce VR components and systems. As the technology is relatively new, the research directions continue to diversify and the competition among different approaches to the design of VR systems continues to shape the technology. Nevertheless, this diversity is continually counteracted by the predominance that some approaches are gaining over others.

As an example of this diversity, we examined different options for the representation of the user's body. The variety of virtual bodies is the product of a number of factors, especially the backgrounds of the labs and the interests and experiences of individual researchers. Yet when we move from this "local" level of individual research institutions to the wider level of VR development in the world at large, a number of other factors come into the foreground. Among commercial VR developers, the prevalence of certain devices (HMD plus flying joystick), for example, or hardware and software constraints (generating a simple virtual body or none at all), play a key role in determining the shape of the virtual body.

The predominance of certain types of virtual bodies should not be taken to imply that commercial forces override the research ideas that are being advanced in the labs. How users feel present in and interact with virtual worlds is crucially dependent on their virtual bodies, and this remains an ongoing issue in VR research. There are also differences between the types of virtual bodies that are suited to different contexts: training for carrying out precise manual tasks in virtual worlds requires a different virtual body, for example, from the type necessary in networked VR for the purpose of communication. As regards virtual bodies, VR research continues to filter into the development of certain devices and contexts of application—and vice versa.

At the same time, it is also the case that VR technology has temporarily congealed in a form whereby the most common shape of virtual bodies is different from those being investigated in the labs. And the point that there continues to be a diversity of representations of virtual bodies against the backdrop of a small number of temporarily congealed or dominant options could equally be made for the development of other components of VR systems, like HMDs, input devices, and software tools.

Some areas of VR technology, as we have seen, have developed more rapidly than others. There has been a vigorous assault on several key reverse salients, especially display resolution, tracking accuracy, and the ability to generate complex graphical virtual worlds. But since no optimal technical design for VR systems has yet established itself, and since the applications domains for VR have not yet been fixed, there is still much scope for variety in the overall shape of VR systems. This variety, however, needs to be placed in the context of the two main areas in which markets for VR are emerging: niches for specialized machines with high-powered and customized specifications, on the one hand, and a mass market for inexpensive entertainment systems, on the other.

As the forces that shape VR systems shift from the former to the latter, they may also be moving away from the "push" of research to the "pull" of market demand. Yet this picture is too simplified: helmets-and-joysticks games are located within a highly competitive and volatile computer games market that is driven by a continual demand for innovation from one generation of games to the next. This is therefore a market both for entertainment games *and* for new technology. Moreover, the "pull" of the market may, in this case, be affected by high expectations as well as fears about the new technology.

At the high end of the market, too, it is not simply a case of technology "push," but also of the fit between the cost of VR systems and the uses to which they are put. Such cost/benefit analyses and comparisons between the performance of VR systems and other devices are increasingly shaping VR R&D, but at this end there is now also a strong institutional momentum to develop high-powered devices in a variety of commercial and noncommercial settings.

The importance of delineating how VR systems have come into being, however, is not just about the genesis of this technology. This summary has merely provided the background for making sense of the emerging patterns of everyday VR use. As an everyday tool, VR systems can be seen as part of a longer-term trend to create more accessible ("user-friendly") means for interacting with computers. Sutherland's "ultimate display" was an early attempt in this direction, but it is only within the last decade or so that the operation of computers by means of manipulating computer-generated images has become commonplace.

A number of technologies have been affected by this trend, including computer-graphics interfaces for personal computers, interactive television, computer games, computer graphics carried via computer-mediated communication, computer-aided design, and other forms of computer modeling. In examining the everyday uses of VR, especially education and games, it has therefore been necessary to place them in this wider context of changing patterns in the use of computers and computer-based technologies.

In education and games, we found that the constraints and possibilities of VR systems depend to a large extent on the user's ability to navigate and manipulate the virtual world rather than to the technical high-poweredness of the VR systems (which is often considered a high priority among VR researchers). Learning by manipulating virtual worlds is, therefore, not so much subject to the constraints of current VR technology, but to finding the places in the curriculum in which this manipulation offers advantages over existing methods of teaching and learning.

Certain areas of learning, as we have seen, were enhanced by the use of VR in the classroom, especially world-building and the ability to move around in a virtual environment. The disadvantages of VR, however, were not so much that virtual worlds cut users off from the world around them—as may be the case with other VR systems that are used on a day-to-day basis and that allow little in the way of creativity and exploration—but that this tool ties learners to a set of skills that it may or may not be possible to build on further.[1]

The educational settings that we have focused on cannot be divorced from the general context of VR development. The most widespread uses of VR for learning are not in secondary schools but in training applications. Here the test of usefulness lies not in the learning process as such, but in the transferability of skills to real-world situations. This is an area that has been dominated by military training and there have so far been only a few attempts at evaluating how performance in this field is influenced by VR (Lampton et al. 1994). The proliferation of educational projects, such as the three we have examined, is therefore hemmed in by the more intensive development of VR for training purposes, on one side—which may make our three pilot projects seem like experimentation for experimentation's sake—and the restricted niche of VR in the curriculum, on the other.

So far, the educational use of VR has been characterized by trial and error rather than through assessment of its usefulness by comparison with that of other technologies or with that of other teaching methods. In the world-at-large, however, VR systems are competing with a large supply of interactive computer technology for education and for "edutainment." In any case, with the exception of some components for special needs education and for military training, VR technology in education has consisted of off-the-shelf systems rather than systems specifically designed for educational purposes. This means that the educational uses of VR are closely tied to the wider proliferation of VR systems. Hence it remains to be seen whether the momentum of these educational projects can be sustained in the future.[2]

The entertainment uses of VR have already been discussed at length. Here we merely need to consider how VR games fit into the overall dynamic of VR development. The first point that can be made is that VR games have become so numerous that they are in many ways now spearheading VR development. Even if researchers in the early 1990s looked skeptically upon the games sector, it is now generally acknowledged that VR games are becoming the first widespread application of the technology (barring the possibility of a moral panic or public expressions of concern over health and safety). By now, all researchers and developers of VR technologies need to take the potential impact of entertainment games into account. For this reason, too, it has been necessary to make a distinction between a high-end professional market and a low-end consumer market for VR systems.

The distinction between the professional and the consumer poles of VR development can be used to make a further point about the overall direction of this technology; namely, that the commercial R&D effort is now, for the most part, directed at entertainment. Conversely, university-based research efforts are mainly aimed at high-end professional VR systems. It is conceivable that the two will converge at some stage or that some components will migrate from one end of VR development to the other. The most common shape of the technology, however, both in terms of its technical features and in terms of public perception, has so far been determined by entertainment systems. This, too, is an area in which, despite the future openness of scientific and technological advance and despite a possible shift toward other areas of application, the process of congealing has begun to set the parameters for the social implications of VR technology.

These two poles also allow us to return to the Weberian perspective on these implications. The high end of VR has extended the range of available visualization tools. This extension of control has taken place in a small number of contexts and has enabled users to engage more directly with the display. And although professional contexts are also those in which advanced computer-related tools are likely to have been in use already, nevertheless, again, VR has advanced beyond these existing technologies in specific ways, inasmuch as phenomena can be realistically modeled and manipulated. The disenchanting side of the effects of VR, in this case, relate to the additional ways in which powerful machine-generated visualization tools are increasingly used within the worlds of scientific research and other professional areas. At the high end of VR, the extension of instrumental rationality and of impersonal control are thus confined to specialists and those who make use of their expertise.

At the other extreme, VR has provided a more sophisticated generation of entertainment attractions. But in this case, the enhanced immersiveness of VR has mainly been placed in the service of existing forms of game play. The additional control over the action undoubtedly increases enjoyment of these games; yet at the same time, VR has extended the way in which artificially generated environments envelop players. To this we can add that unlike the VR of the specialist machines at the high end, VR in entertainment is making inroads into a large market and a popular pastime. It may be the case that what happens in the world of entertainment is not as significant as what happens in the workday world of, say, medical technology. There is, nevertheless, considerable importance in the fact that leisure-seekers increasingly spend their time in ever more engrossing technologically-mediated environments.

At this stage we can shift from a dynamic account of VR to a more static and structural one that relates VR to the different spheres of social life. This will allow us to emphasize that VR has followed a trajectory that has, to some extent, been independent of social forces (and that for this reason, a realist standpoint is warranted in relation to scientific and technological advance). We shall therefore briefly consider the relation between VR development and the spheres of politics, culture, and economics.

The politics of the VR research effort have not been confined within national borders. As we have seen, some of the most successful VR systems—from a technical or a commercial viewpoint—have been developed through alliances between firms and research centers in different countries. And although government agencies and national advisory bodies have sought to harness a lead in VR technology for the sake of economic advantage, the advance of VR technology has for the most part remained outside the orbit of their efforts and recommendations. Moreover, the financial support from governments for R&D efforts has only had a limited impact. It remains to be seen whether the possible exceptions here—military funding for networked VR in the United States, the national program for VR-related telecommunications and manufacturing technology in Japan, and the European Community's networked VR efforts—will confound this assessment. In any case, the efforts of researchers, entrepreneurs, and government officials to stimulate publicly-funded projects with a view to gaining an unassailable lead in the field seem to be receding in importance behind the concrete problem of developing successful or marketable systems.

If, however, we understand by the politics of artifacts the attempts to set standards for technologies that in this way remain locked in, then, again, the efforts of institutions to assert the superiority of their approach to VR—and thereby dominate the VR effort—have been unsuccessful. The cutting edge of VR R&D continues to be dispersed among a handful of research centers, as well as among powerful commercial players, and there also continues to be a rivalry between divergent views about technologically superior approaches. A further way to approach the politics of new technologies might be to emphasize the conservative implications of the growing divide between those who have access to technology and those who do not. But whether this can be applied to VR remains to be seen.[3]

The main feature of VR development in the sphere of culture is a group of far-fetched ideas about its potential impact. The promoters of VR technology have benefited from the publicity surrounding VR and from the enthusiasm about new ICTs generally. At the same time, they have also sought to distance themselves from VR games and from cyberculture because of the need for a "serious" image for their efforts. Nevertheless, apart from in media coverage, the worlds of cyberculture and of VR R&D have had few points of contact. Thus, the fears of some VR researchers that publicity from the "frivolous" side of VR would undermine their "seriousness," or the fears of cybercultural enthusiasts that the R&D establishment would "hijack" the technology for its own ends, have both proved unfounded.

The economics of VR can be divided into the resources for VR research, on the one hand, and the markets for VR systems and components, on the other. As we have seen, the number of VR research centers has grown rapidly and with them the number of new VR projects. The funding for VR research, which has come from industry, the military, and academic institutions, has kept pace with this growth and diversification of the research effort. More recently, the resources of the consumer electronics industry have come into the foreground. The growth of the consumer end of VR is important, as the balance between the spending required on VR R&D, measured against the value of the market for VR, is beginning to tilt toward the latter.

The worldwide market for VR systems and components remains on the scale of several hundred million dollars, but a firm place has by now been established for research-related and other visualization tools and entertainment products. The commercial viability of domestic VR systems is about to be tested in the highly competitive computer games market, which is worth billions of dollars per year. But as VR is largely an untried technology, consumer preferences may not be the only decisive factor: moral panics and fears of addiction, for example, may play an unforeseeable role. Nevertheless, by comparison with VR for scientific research and other "high-end" applications, which remain relatively insulated from the competition of the market, VR consumer electronics are more open to the external environment that will therefore shape—even if it does not determine—the direction of the technology (see also Cawson, Haddon, and Miles 1995).

To sum up, the political and cultural influences on VR have been marginal. However, economic forces are playing an increasing role in VR development. But this, as we saw earlier, is not a simple case of the "push" of technology or the "pull" of the market. The crucial role in VR development has been the momentum generated by the research institutions that have refined VR systems and extended their capacity as tools for manipulating virtual worlds.[4] This momentum is now in place, so that the "realism" of scientific and technological advance has begun to establish particular tracks; namely, those pertaining to the key scientific and technological hurdles of VR systems. On the applications side, too, the forces shaping VR development, as we have seen, are not just economic ones. Instead, it is a question of situating the "local" contexts in which VR has come to be used within a larger framework of technological advance and of the factors affecting the proliferation of VR systems (which are to a large extent economic ones).

This point applies not only to the social forces shaping VR but also to the social implications of this technology. The consequences of the day-to-day uses of VR are not merely cultural, political, and economic ones (although this may also be the case if, for example, VR systems enhance productivity).[5] There are also technological consequences for social life in the sense that the social world is increasingly populated by tools that mediate our relationship with the natural and social environments. In other words, technological advance (like scientific advance) is cumulative, but this advance has to be translated into the contribution that it makes to the process of extending instrumental rationality and disenchantment.

In the case of VR, this process has mainly taken place in the areas of professional and entertainment applications in which this technology adds to the tools that we use—with different implications in each. And again, although the contribution that VR has made to the social role of technologies has so far been on a relatively small scale, it is nevertheless particularly in the early uses of new technologies that we can recognize this contribution as a distinctive and autonomous one.

Information or Communication Technology?

One question that is raised in identifying the place of VR in social life is about where it fits into the everyday uses of existing tools. Ellis, for example, has suggested that virtual environments are "communications media."[6] It would be misleading, however, to think of all VR applications in this way. The notion of a communications technology normally implies that two or more people are involved and that the emphasis is placed on the messages that pass between them.[7] Similarly, a "medium" requires at least two participants—except that in this case, the stress may be on the tool that carries the message. The notion of "information" contained in "information technology," however, can imply conveying something to a single person rather than an exchange between people.

Single-user VR systems can therefore be regarded as an information technology. If this is correct, it follows that the terms "communication" and "medium" should only be used in the context of multiuser VR. The exception might be cases in which the *content* of VR has been shaped by other media, the main example being VR games that take their themes from films or from other computer games. If, however, VR can be seen as a medium only in these cases, the reverse is also instructive—namely, that apart from this, VR cannot simply be seen as yet another medium that delivers the same content by other means.

Nevertheless, when VR *is* a communications medium in a multiuser configuration, it means, as Palmer points out, that VR "can be evaluated as a medium of interpersonal communication in the same way all media have been evaluated" (1995:291). In other words, it will be possible to ask, for example, how effectively messages are conveyed in VR. Such evaluations have not so far taken place since networked VR has not been used extensively enough, but it is clear that one of the key differences between VR and other communications media, from this perspective, are the sensory channels involved.

The auditory channel in VR is not very different from that used in existing technologies such as the telephone, and neither, in practice, are the other nonvisual channels of VR technology, since, for example, teletouch in a multiparticipant virtual environment has not yet been used. The visual channel is the obvious exception. There is a fundamental difference between visual channels in VR and in existing technologies such as videophones or computer-mediated communication that incorporates 2-D graphics, given that VR provides a manipulable and navigable space in which communication takes place.

The precise differences between this form of communication and existing ones, however, are bound to vary and depend, for example, on the representation of users and on the manipulability of the environment. These differences are nevertheless likely to be striking, because the disadvantages of multiuser VR (such as the awkwardness of dealing with virtual representations of others) and the benefits (the joint manipulation of a navigable virtual environment) potentially amplify the costs and benefits of existing communication tools in a way that is similar to the introduction of other new mass media. Palmer has remarked that "advances in communication technologies have been useful in closing distance and time, but on the whole tend to remove individuals from direct access to behavioral transactions in which multiple verbal and nonverbal cues are interactively and transparently orchestrated in real time" (1995:286). This statement may also apply to networked VR, but the paucity of "direct access" in VR must be weighed against the fact that this mode of communication takes place in an information-rich visual environment that sets VR apart from existing communications tools.

A different way of seeing VR as a communications technology is by reference to the notion of "interactivity." This line of argument has been taken by Rafaeli (1988). Yet the notion of "interactivity" only makes sense when both parties to the action are specified, whether they are people or machines. These are relationships that we have explored in detail in the various contexts in which VR is used, and it is not clear that "interaction" in general adds anything over and above the specific types of interaction that we have analyzed.[8]

Rafaeli, nevertheless, argues that the model of direct human-human communication should not be taken as the standard against which mediated (i.e., human-machine) communication is measured, and hence that machine responsiveness to humans can also be considered a form of communicative action. This implies that a single user of a machine could be seen as being engaged in communication—as long as the machine is responsive. Against this view, it can pointed out that information and communication technologies as classes of objects do not establish relationships with humans, even if humans may establish relationships of sorts with machines (and, "through" machines, with other people).

Another way of making this point is to emphasize that Rafaeli's notion of interactivity is based on the idea of the responsiveness to earlier messages or references, so that there is a continual feedback chain between the person and an other (i.e., a machine) in terms of the "incorporation" of earlier references (1988:119). Inasmuch as the virtual world constantly responds to the user, this type of feedback clearly applies to VR. Rafaeli then goes on to say that psychologists would have little difficulty in studying this kind of human-machine phenomenon, which can often be measured in seconds, whereas sociologists *would* have difficulties with it, as they are typically concerned with longer-term patterns.

Yet this reasoning misconstrues the issue: If we assume that people interact a great deal with (an interactive version of) television or with computers—in Rafaeli's sense in which they modify each other iteratively—does the interaction imply that the medium or the technology eventually establishes a mutual relationship with people? The experience with what might be called interactive tools or media so far—if we think, for example, of interactive television, computer games, single-user VR, or similar technologies—suggests that no *mutual* relationship exists. It may be the case that people desire or prefer interactivity in their machines, as Rafaeli's questionnaire findings indicate (1988:122–126), but that does not mean that they have somehow become more responsive to interactive technologies than to noninteractive technologies over the long term—or, to put it differently—that they have made them more part of their lives or ingested (so to speak) the responsiveness of the medium.

For users to incorporate interactive technologies into their lives in Rafaeli's sense, users would have to have "become" more interactive with certain types of technologies in everyday life, or the technologies would have to have become more interactive in response to them. But this eventuality is currently so far removed from our actual use of new technologies that we can safely ignore it from the point of view of our analysis of VR and other ICTs.

One of the reasons for discussing concepts like communication and interaction in such depth is that they bear directly on the central theoretical issue of this book—the social implications of new technologies. Many claims and counterclaims have been made about possible changes in our lives stemming from new ICTs. One of these claims is that new computer-based technologies will allow new modes of interaction and communication with machines.

In the 1950s and 1960s, for example, it used to be the case that people referred to "operating" computers, whereas nowadays we "interact" with them. The upshot of the discussion in the preceding paragraphs is that we in fact still "operate" VR systems, but we do so in a way that differs significantly from previous and other uses of ICTs. These differences, as we have seen, cannot be divorced from their social contexts, and the relevant contexts that apply to VR are those in which VR is used as a tool in entertainment, in visual computing, and in training and education. Put differently, the way in which technological artifacts have been refined and allow us to manipulate the world—and thus how they have extended instrumental rationality—is as a particular kind of technology in specific contexts and not as a general force that can be divorced from these contexts.

Enchanted and Disenchanted Worlds

VR has precipitated so many ideas about its potential impact largely because of the possibility of its extensive use as a communications medium. Biocca, for example, takes the view that "time spent in using this immersive medium may be higher than for any previous medium. Kubey and Csikszentmihalyi estimated that people spend approximately seven years of their life watching television. If people eventually use VR technology for the same amount of time that they spend watching television and using computers, some users could spend twenty or more years 'inside' virtual reality."[9]

This vastly overstates the potential influence of VR. VR will not replace existing ICTs, but rather complement and add to them. As Rogers has pointed out, the history of communications technologies is "cumulative," but "each successive technology did not replace previous communication media (although it usually affected them in important ways). So the history of communication is the story of 'more.' Each new medium may change the function of previous media, but they do not disappear" (1986:26). The same could be said about the history of information technologies, and it is easy for us to see now that the limited niche that VR occupies among ICTs as a professional and entertainment tool fits this pattern of complementing some technologies and transforming others—without the need to stipulate the disappearance of computers and television as we know them.

It may be useful to look at this another way: it has been suggested that information and communication technologies will converge, so that, for example, computers and television could become one machine. The implications of this are said to be that the nature of television and computing will change beyond recognition. It seems more likely, however, that even a computer-controlled television will be confined to the living room and feature mainly entertainment, whereas a computer with television images is more likely to keep its place in the study and be used for work, even if each in the future contains more of the elements of the other and they are both hooked up to a two-way telecommunications network.[10]

In a similar way, we can now say that users are more likely to put on VR helmets (or VR glasses) and use navigation devices in some contexts—among them public entertainment arcades, professional visualization facilities, military training facilities, and schools—rather than others. As concerns the additional space that VR may come to occupy in the living room, the introduction of VR to the home has only just begun and it remains to be seen whether it will become a permanent or popular one.

These limitations also place other far-reaching ideas about ICTs in perspective. For example, U.S. vice-president Al Gore, perhaps the key politician currently shaping U.S. policy on ICTs, chaired a Senate subcommittee hearing on VR in May 1992.[11] Much was made at this hearing about the competition between the United States and Japan, with Gore suggesting that without government action, the economic benefits of the American lead in research would be lost to other countries that were developing practical applications, as had happened in other instances.[12]

In Gore's view, an information superhighway (or a computer network infrastructure) will be essential to the future well-being of the United States, and VR plays a key role in this: "If the users of virtual reality could be at some distance from these [graphics] engines and use them by means of an information superhighway, a network in other words, then that would potentially speed up the introduction of new applications for this new technology" (Gore quoted by Wiseman 1992:8–9). This network, in turn, "would enable a child to come home from school and, instead of playing Nintendo, use something that looks like a video game machine to plug into the Library of Congress" (1991:110). So far, however, there has been no VR link to the Library of Congress, and Nintendo's Virtual Boy, a game that is similar to existing computer games, has become the first mass-produced domestic VR game system to come onto the market.[13]

Jaron Lanier has also speculated about the possibilities of communication by means of shared virtual environments. He believes, for example, that multiuser VR may have positive and negative aspects, allowing human beings to share their ideas and dreams, on the one hand, or absorbing them within their own private world, like television or video games, on the other (Lanier 1989:9; see also Lanier and Biocca 1992:156).

One possibility is that shared VR could recreate a sense of community that has been lost with the increasing isolation of the individual. Thus he contrasts "California [which] is the worst example of this. Individuals don't even meet on the sidewalks anymore. We live in our cars," with the "English commons, where there's a shared community space" (Lanier and Biocca 1992:157).

He also advocates that children up to the age of eight or ten should in the future not be allowed to use VR, although this "could be framed positively. There could be a nice sort of ritual for kids when they get old enough to use simulators" (Lanier and Biocca 1992:168). Meanwhile, however, the Nintendo game that has just been mentioned and other VR games can be purchased without ritual by children of any age, and so far they offer single-user action adventures rather than sharing dreams on an English common.

Futuristic ideas about shared virtual worlds overlook the fact that current communications networks present considerable obstacles for VR, both technical and social. Whereas local VR networks do not present problems of bandwidth, more extensive networks are faced with the technical limitation that long-distance networks, with enough bandwidth to carry complex virtual worlds, are only just becoming feasible, and similarly, that the social momentum for networking large numbers of offices and homes is only just emerging.

Hence shared virtual worlds, which may in the future carry the social implications that have been catalogued here much further, are currently confined to the pilot projects of researchers and the military. These projects and the computer-mediated communication tools already available on the Internet and via telephone lines—such as multiuser dungeons, Habitat, and VRML—provide the closest equivalent for the foreseeable future for gauging the social implications of shared virtual worlds.[14] In the meantime, the social implications of existing shared virtual worlds have congealed around the engrossing experiences of VR games (which, even in a local network configuration, do not represent a vast leap from existing computer games), as well as the additional capabilities of shared visualization tools, which are still at the prototype stage.

If, instead of trying to imagine the future, we wish to identify the current implications of VR (which may, of course, give some indication about its prospects), then, as I argued in Chapter 1, the thrust of the social implications of new technologies should be sought where technological and social developments converge. Thus the low-cost systems for the entertainment games market are technically relatively unsophisticated because they have to compete in price with other arcade-style and home computer games. For this reason, these games also need to offer a highly immersive experience and thus tend to follow the format of existing games. VR games have therefore tended to be short—up to 5 minutes or so—and because they have mainly been played in arcades, they have also typically been one-off experiences.

In the case of networked games, the short length of play has placed limits on the sense of competition or cooperation with other players. The technology and the use to which it is put are therefore fairly well-matched: an action-adventure game does not require much more power than an ordinary personal computer and the low-resolution display offers detail that is comparable with that of other computer games. Likewise, the level of interaction with the virtual world—the user moves around in a rudimentary landscape and shoots things—does not require a great leap in level of detail or computing power.

It is true that VR games have advanced significantly in a short time, so that, for example, HMDs have become much lighter and offer improved resolution. The level of detail of virtual worlds has also improved dramatically through computer graphics techniques such as texturing and shading, and these and other improvements in technical sophistication are likely to continue since non-VR computer games are also becoming more sophisticated in offering three-dimensional perspectives and more realistic graphics.

It is also conceivable that low-cost VR systems may push VR in new directions by making the technology much more widely available, just as personal computers brought computing to a much wider audience, which then, in turn, transformed the nature of computing.[15] But with this important exception, games have at this stage already lent VR technology a particular shape—the combination of low-resolution HMD, flying joystick, and minimally interactive and cartoonlike virtual worlds.

VR games are similar to existing computer games, but there is also a difference. A common image of computer games is of a child transfixed in front of the screen for hours on end. And yet computer games also involve parents and friends with whom coplay and access to the games need to be negotiated and where roles (such as "the expert") and relations (for example, parents using game play as a reward) establish patterns around the games. VR games are too short and have not yet entered the household sufficiently to establish these patterns, but if the several VR games that are currently being developed for domestic use were to become widespread, an important difference between them and existing computer games would be that players are much more cut off from the world around them.

As we have seen, VR games machines are much less sophisticated in terms of interaction than high-powered VR systems. Whether, in spite of this, VR games will nevertheless be more absorbing than other computer games is difficult to say, since this will vary with the technology and the content of the games. In any case, VR games cut players off from their surroundings and give them a more direct sense of interacting with a computer-generated world, and in this sense, they intensify the involvement of players and extend the capacity of existing games machines.

At the other extreme, the various relatively expensive VR systems aimed at more specialized markets are devices that are tailored to particular tasks. Hence, there is a variety of systems and components and it is likely this variety will remain at the "high" end. In spite of the diversity of systems, it is possible to venture some comments that apply generally to nonentertainment VR: one is that outside the realm of the most high-powered systems for research, there is intense competition among producers of commercially-available VR systems to create robust and comfortable machines that combine high-resolution displays with easy-to-use navigational devices. This is because if VR is not simply to be used as an experimental or demonstration tool, it needs to be accessible and flexible enough to suit workaday settings and cater to users who are not computer specialists. The second point is that in spite of the differences with VR games, the most common type of system is nevertheless the combination of an HMD and a flying 3-D mouse, although, in this case, these two components and the computing hardware and software are of a different order of sophistication compared with VR games.

If this last point seems to bring nongame and game VR systems closer together, it needs to be emphasized that the difference between the two is greater than it may appear because of what users can *do* with these systems. More expensive and technically sophisticated VR systems often allow the virtual world to be modified by programming the software. They also allow tasks to be carried out in the virtual world that require precise tracking and a greater degree of control over the "objects."[16] In sum, these devices allow the user to explore and manipulate an information-rich virtual environment. The reason for emphasizing this is that these are precisely the features that set VR technology apart from other, similar information and communication technologies.

Nonentertainment VR systems can be compared with the types of tools used in medical research, training, architecture, and the like. The vast majority of existing VR systems in these contexts are used for visualizing objects or environments that are difficult or impossible to visualize with conventional tools. What they have in common compared with non-VR systems is not so much that this visualization is more "realistic" than with other machines (although that is often the case) but rather that a different kind of control over the image or the environment is made possible, especially in terms of being able to move around objects and to change them.

Again, these capabilities need to be put in the context that these visualization tools are mostly prototypes, that they are mostly used for short periods, and that the devices are often cumbersome and have not yet been fine-tuned for comfort and ease of navigation. Within these constraints, VR systems allow the user to carry out tasks related to the visualization of objects and environments that cannot be achieved in the same way with similar tools. The limitations of current systems should therefore not obscure the fact that in terms of visualization and especially interaction with virtual worlds, VR extends the capabilities of other available machines.

As far as networked VR systems are concerned, apart from locally networked games and military training, there have so far been only a handful of demonstration projects, and it is as yet unclear what kinds of cooperative tasks or activities shared virtual worlds are suited for. Here, again, the comparisons are with conventional tools for computer-supported cooperative work, videophones, and games such as multiuser dungeons and Habitat. But since no common mode of "copresence" in virtual worlds has established itself, it is difficult to foresee what kinds of interpersonal relations will emerge in networked environments and what kind of "fit" there might be between networked VR and other communications tools.

Before we can draw these points together, one further capability of VR systems deserves comment, and that is world-building. Creating virtual worlds, which normally takes place on a desktop computer as opposed to inside the virtual environment itself, is relatively easy. We saw, for example, that in the West Denton and HITLab education projects, complex and imaginative virtual worlds were built within a matter of days and with relatively little help from teachers. The same is true of virtual world design in other contexts, such as among those who develop VR systems: here, too, the task of world-building mainly requires good design skills rather than computer programming skills (Giles 1994). As VR software often includes world-building capabilities (sometimes referred to as "world-authoring kits"), it is not difficult for the lay person to master the design of virtual worlds by means of drawing and design tools. In this sense, too, VR extends the capacity of existing tools for creating computer-generated worlds because it essentially combines the ease-of-use of computer-aided design software with the complexities of worlds that have so far been confined to simulator technology.

The degree to which VR systems are used for building virtual worlds compared with consumers' use of ready-made virtual worlds, however, is still very much in the balance. A number of VR systems offer world-building capabilities, mostly on a desktop computer, but in some cases also from within the virtual world.[17] These systems are technically not much more demanding or more expensive than VR systems with ready-built worlds or those that require professional skills. Up until now, however, building virtual worlds has not been commonplace except in research and development. With the proliferation of VR systems, the question of whether creating virtual worlds rather than experiencing ready-made worlds (which is mainly to do with software rather than hardware) becomes more widespread will be crucial for the future shape of the technology.

The social implications of VR in terms of rationalization and disenchantment can now be summarized as follows: VR systems extend the instrumental control that we have over computer-generated worlds, be they for entertainment, professional work, or communicative interaction at a distance. By the same token, the systems add to the technologically-mediated environments we spend time in. And although these consequences are limited to particular settings, they enhance the manipulability of virtual worlds and at the same time compel users to occupy purpose-built virtual worlds that engross the senses. Hence, as with other technologies, increasing mastery over the social and natural worlds goes hand in hand with the routine use of man-made environments.

This brings us back to the issues in the sociology of technologies that were raised at the outset of this study. The emergence and the implications of new technologies, as we can now see, are closely related; as particular technological directions become dominant, so too, do the ways in which technologies are used. In the introduction, I argued that a conception of the autonomy of scientific and technological advance, or "realism," is essential to our understanding of the emergence of new technologies like VR. This autonomy has been demonstrated by reference to the enhanced capabilities of VR systems. Insofar as these systems extend instrumental rationality, they do so in different ways in different areas of social life. Thus, for example, the implications of VR for the world of entertainment differ from those pertaining to the world of professional visualization.

In addition, we have seen that where social factors have been most important in shaping the implications of VR, they have mainly been economic ones. This emphasis on the relationship between technological and economic forces sets this study apart from the "social shaping" approach to new technologies, in which the focus has been almost entirely on the cultural and political shaping of new technologies. But the argument has also departed from the approach to new technologies in economics that mainly deals with the macro level and gives priority to economically driven innovation and economic demand. This study, by contrast, has attempted to interrelate technological and social forces at a number of levels and to identify the concrete forces that have shaped VR in various settings as well as its (noneconomic) social implications.

One area in which this study has remained open-ended, at least in terms of current or ongoing developments, is in making the link between the wider level—at which what counts is the proliferation of VR systems—and the local level, at which VR has been put to various concrete uses. We can now see that the implications of VR for social life are suspended somewhere between these two levels and that the central thrust of the social role of VR technology depends on both— or rather, on the connections between them.

It might now be possible to draw these connections together more closely, detailing the degree to which transformations in the technology and in social relations on the local level add up to larger changes—and vice versa, how larger technological and social changes affect the various local contexts. But for new technologies, these interrelations are fluid, both because of the ongoing possibilities created by scientific and technological advance and because the fit between artifacts and their applications easily becomes reconfigured.

If we now attempted to gauge more precisely how the sum of the local implications of the technology and the effects of its wider proliferation mesh together, then we might be able to venture into the realm of forecasting future applications and consequences of VR. But the main purpose of this study has been to define the major outlines of the conjunction between technological advances and social implications to date, and whereas this may provide a framework for thinking about the options that lie ahead, it does not allow us to make predictions.

In spite of what has just been said, it may be useful to reflect briefly on the wider influence of information technologies or electronic media on society in order to think about how the limited implications of VR (which have so far been on a relatively small scale) might eventually fit into a larger picture. To do this, we can briefly consider two quite different perspectives, one from the social sciences and the other from the humanities. These ideas will lead beyond the conclusions that have been presented so far, but perhaps that is no bad thing in a study that has attempted to stick to the very narrow subject matter of a single new technology.

One way to approach the question of how ICTs are changing our lives is to see these effects as part of a more long-term pattern. Meyrowitz's *No Sense of Place: The Impact of Electronic Media on Social Behavior* provides a good example. The author sees the increasing use of electronic media as part of a shift away from print culture and toward an electronic society. Along these lines, he forecasts that "the increasingly sophisticated use of interactive computer graphics and the drive toward computers that can understand and use human speech, both suggest that mastery of literacy may soon be as irrelevant to the basic operation of computers and computer-controlled machines as it is to the operation of television sets and automobiles" (1985:328). He also suggests that the widespread use of electronic media is breaking down boundaries and hierarchies in society[18]:

> Like television, the video game does not divide its "audience" into different ages. People of all ages play the games. Further, age and traditional education do not have any direct effect on the level of skills. Indeed, many young children master games their parents cannot even fathom. Many video games involve multiple lines of action, increasing speed, and increasing rate of increasing speed. These aspects are all foreign to the one-thing-at-a-time, one-thing-after-another, and take-time-to-think world of reading. (1985:326)

This passage resonates with several of the most common features of VR that we have identified, particularly when we think about the skills required for creating and navigating virtual worlds. Whether VR contributes to the shift that Meyrowitz describes is an open question, but perhaps we can glimpse VR here as part of a wider social transformation.

Meyrowitz's way of thinking about electronic media is mainly based on sociology and psychology. A completely different perspective, this time from the humanities, is offered by Gifford's *The Farther Shore: A Natural History of Perception, 1798–1984*, even though he deals with a similar subject matter and time frame. For Gifford, sight is the "queen of the senses" (1991:1) and he points out that there has been a "flood of new technologies . . . of eye extenders and modifiers over the last 150 years" (1991:40). It would be easy to see VR as part of the most recent wave in this flood.

Be that as it may, here is his conclusion about how these technologies have affected our everyday lives:

> In this transformation of the . . . eye, our eyes are under siege, overloaded with visual riches until we're in danger of being distracted into a sort of visual paralysis, our ability to discriminate homogenized and dulled by surfeit. The corollary symptoms are all around us. Advertising and the arts are dominated by visual stunts designed to override our distraction, and the critics among us compensate for the homogenization with a rage to discriminate, a rush to judgement and an abrupt stridency of tone that announce the poverty that threatens us in the midst of plenty. (1991:46)

Again, there is much here that seems to ring true for VR, especially if we think about the link between the richness of the visual display in VR and the difficulty that we might have, in our capacity as "critics," to maintain a sense of balance about its implications.

This is a good place to lower our sights and attempt to draw together some of the more limited lessons that can be derived from VR. I have argued that the social implications of new technologies consist conjointly of scientific and technological advances and of the spread of instrumental rationality throughout the social world. The limitations of how VR contributes to this process are due to the fact that VR has gained a confined place among the computer-based ICTs that we use. So far, VR systems have mainly been used in entertainment, in training, and in visual computing for professional applications. In these areas, VR technology has evolved from a prototype into an everyday tool, but it has yet to replace existing tools in these areas or to take its full place as a complement to them. At the same time, VR has extended the way in which realistic computer-generated worlds can be manipulated and in this way it has surpassed the technologies that were previously used in these domains.

Apart from stand-alone machines, the exploitation of networked VR, as we have seen, is technically much more demanding. But although there are currently far fewer networked VR systems than stand-alone machines, the potential for the proliferation of VR systems in this case is much greater, since shared virtual worlds add the benefits of communication to those of VR. VR as a networked communication tool would multiply the effect of the kinds of extensions of instrumental rationality that we have attributed to VR. Existing modes of computer-mediated communication are predominantly text-based, but the creation of shared virtual worlds that are mainly visual paves the way for incorporating 3-D spaces and visual representations of users within these communication networks.

With regard to content, we have seen that virtual worlds span the range of imaginary and realistic worlds. On both fronts, VR software has extended the range of objects that can be found in computer-generated worlds. In other words, the frontier of imaginary and realistic virtual real estate has been continuously expanding. This real estate consists for the most part of representations of the built environment or of things that cannot easily be displayed with conventional means. The fact that VR systems have become more widespread has meant that the need exists for an ever greater range of objects within virtual worlds. However this process continues, the content of virtual worlds has enlarged the scope of manipulable, mainly visual, computer-generated environments.

At this time, the future proliferation of VR systems depends mainly on the institutional momentum that has gathered behind their development and on the price and performance of these systems compared with other machines. In assessing the social dynamic of new technologies, however, this proliferation—or diffusion—is only one part of the equation. New technologies also set new technological and social benchmarks in the use of artifacts. As we have seen, VR systems have extended the capabilities of existing machines to the extent that the worlds of computer gaming have become an experience that engrosses the user's senses—and in professional visual computing for which VR has created more manipulable and realistic models.

By enlarging the scope of how we use computers, VR systems have added worlds, both imaginary and realistic, to our repertoire of tools. These worlds combine instrumental rationality and the impersonality of the external conditions of life insofar as they enhance our control over the world and at the same time add to the man-made environments that envelop our senses. The balance between the two, between worlds that can be modified and enrich us, as against those that divert and dull our perception, lies with tomorrow's worlds, both virtual and social.

Notes

Chapter 1

1. Beniger (1986:1–27) offers an overview of various conceptions of the "information society" and related concepts.

2. For the "sociology of scientific knowledge," see, for example, Woolgar (1988). Recent approaches to the sociology of technology are brought together in the collections of essays edited by MacKenzie and Wajcman (1985) and Bijker, Hughes, and Pinch (1987). There are many rival strands within the sociology of science and technology that need not concern us here. Randall Collins has noted (in conversation) that although the study of science and technology is still a relatively small, specialized area within sociology, it contains more schools—one might also say "sects"—with competing viewpoints than any other.

3. Overviews of these debates in relation to science are presented in Collins and Restivo (1983) and Restivo (1994). For new technologies, the collection edited by Dierkes and Hoffmann (1992) represents a useful survey.

4. See Mokyr (1990:151–192 and 273–304). A selection of recent contributions to this debate can be found in Smith and Marx (1994).

5. Much of the discussion in this area has focused on science rather than technology, but Woolgar (1991), for example, has argued that technology should be treated as a "text."

6. Price has argued, in a similar vein, that the concepts of science and technology are closely linked (1975:117–135).

7. For an account of computer systems development that focuses on the organizational level, see Friedman (1989).

8. See Schroeder (1995a) and Brubaker (1984:esp. 29–35). Hard (1994) also offers a Weberian analysis of science and technology.

Chapter 2

1. This source of funding, incidentally, is also the main basis of other technologies that have recently gained prominence, electronic mail and the Internet (see Rheingold 1994:esp. 65–109).

2. Systems that allow users to look at the computer-generated display and the real world simultaneously have since become known as "augmented reality displays" (Barfield, Rosenberg, and Lotens 1995).

3. Another machine of a different type that predated Sutherland's was the Headsight system. This device, which was to be used for dangerous remote operations, allowed users to get a sense of being in a remote location by controlling a television camera by means of a head-mounted display that showed images recorded by the camera (Kalawsky 1993:20).

4. Exceptions here are the interactive Mandala games, which are featured in Chapter 4.

5. The history of the close relationship between art and computer graphics technology is charted by Auzenne (1994) and by Darley (1990).

6. See Pausch, Crea, and Conway (1992). The prevailing, though by no means uncontested, theory in this area is the sensory conflict theory put forward by Oman (1991). These issues will be discussed further in Chapter 4.

7. Stytz (1994). Sterling (1993) has suggested that the line between the illusion of military simulation and the reality of war is impossible to draw. This kind of confusion, based on the idea that VR will one day become indistinguishable from reality, is one that we shall encounter elsewhere. Nevertheless, Sterling rightly points to the fact that there is a large market for military simulation, $2.5 billion per year for 1993, in his estimation (1993:96).

8. These differences between VR and other technologies will be discussed later in the book.

9. Rheingold's (1991) *Virtual Reality* provides an overview of the individuals behind the early work on VR. A chronicle of other technical milestones can be found in Kalawsky (1993:17–42) and Ellis (1991). The history of VR is discussed from the perspective of the study of media and communications by Halbach (1994).

10. Tesler (1991). See also Edwards (1994:269–270).

11. This pattern of invention in America is described by Hughes (1989:esp. 1–95).

12. The most extensive technical surveys to date are Kalawsky (1993), Durlach and Mavor (1995), and Barfield and Furness (1995). The book by Burdea and Coiffet (1994) contains useful material on force-feedback devices. The most recent research can be found in the academic journal *Presence: Teleoperators and Virtual Environments,* and the newsletter *VR News* contains up-to-date information about the major manufacturers and commercial issues. There is also a separate *VR News* publication with reports about patents.

13. For the notion of "reverse salients," see Hughes (1987:73). Hughes prefers this notion to that of bottleneck, because the latter is too "rigid," whereas "reverse salient . . . suggests uneven and complex change" (1987:73). But in VR systems, it is not that clear that if one component lags behind the others, the whole system will be affected, as in Hughes's "large

technological systems." Bearing this in mind, we can continue to use Hughes's reverse salient as "components in the system that have fallen behind or are out of phase with the others"(1987: 73).

14. Virtual "environment" and virtual "world" will be used interchangeably, although researchers generally prefer virtual "environment."

15. Researchers point out that the figures given for image resolution are often inflated somewhat because different manufacturers use different specifications (for example, Biocca and Delaney, 1995:76). It should also be mentioned that the quality of the display, as far as the user is concerned, depends not only on the capacities of the VR system but also on the complexity of the virtual world.

16. A television in the United States contains approximately 200,000 pixels (see, for example, Monaco [1981:51]). Virtual environments need to display more information since they consist of dynamic 3-D images that can be manipulated by the user, but TV and VR are also difficult to compare since HMD screens are immediately in front of the eye.

17. *VR News*, vol. 4, issue 4, May 1995.

18. The term that has been coined for the way sound reaches the ears is head-related transfer function, or HRTF (Wenzel 1992). Wenzel points out that different users have different HRTFs and thus auditory displays may need to be tailored to individual users. Most VR systems, however, do not customize their auditory displays in this way.

19. Meyer et al. (1992) provide a survey of tracking devices. Eye-tracking technology, which allows the user's eye movement to control the display, is a technology that is still in its infancy, although researchers are actively investigating its uses for VR (Jacob 1995).

20. Ultimately, it may be possible to build a completely portable VR system. This would require a portable computer and perhaps some combination of gravimetric sensors, accelerometers, and geographical information systems.

21. One of the reasons for having trackers only on two points, on the head and hand, is that multiple point tracking can incur significant lags when used with current technology.

22. The terms "hand-held" and "flying," and also "3-D mouse" or "joystick," will be used interchangeably. It should also be mentioned that some of the joysticks or 3-D mice that will be described can be used in a deskbound mode and, thus, are transformed into conventional 2-D mice or joysticks.

23. Many books on VR, by such authors as Durlach and Mavor (1995), Burdea and Coiffet (1994) and Biocca and Delaney (1995) contain sections on voice recognition.

24. The exception is if the voices of the users need to be realistically localized in the three-dimensional auditory environment, which involves additional computational demands.

25. Heilig's Sensorama, by contrast, included smell, for example.

26. With Sketchpad (a predecessor to the "ultimate display"), as Palfreman and Swade point out, "Sutherland had invented the field of computer graphics 20 years early"(1991:96).

27. Interview with Ian Andrew, managing director of Dimension (now Superscape), July 16, 1992.

28. This statement is somewhat oversimplified since the requirements for local area network speed depend on the complexity of the virtual world and the interaction within it. But there are other local area network technologies that achieve higher speeds. See Durlach and Mavor (1995:366).

29. The National Research Council report (Durlach and Mavor 1995) identifies many areas in great need of research, including several that have only been mentioned briefly here, like force-feedback or input from eye-tracking. The authors' demand for more research can be explained by the fact that this report has as its constituency a large number of labs working on a range of VR issues. Hence, it is not surprising that the report strongly advocates further research in many areas. It is worth mentioning the typical chapter style of the report: as in many academic papers on VR, chapters begin by sketching what is ideally required in a particular area of VR research and end by giving an indication of (as it is put, on one occasion) "what we can get away with" (1995:181) to produce a reasonable VR system.

Chapter Three

1. There are various schemas for periodizing the emergence of new technologies. For an overview, see Rammert (1992:esp. 65).

2. A list of institutions developing VR, including their size and main areas of interest, can be found in Helsel and DeNoble Doherty (1992) and Thompson (1993). The research at the two American institutions is also described in Kalawsky (1993) and Durlach and Mavor (1995).

3. All four institutions are in fact engaged in a range of VR projects, but two areas for which each lab is well-known have been singled out.

4. It is difficult to estimate the number of staff connected with VR at these laboratories, since researchers are also often engaged in non-VR activities. Similarly, it is difficult to assess the level of funding devoted to VR research, both because the VR laboratories are situated within larger institutions and because other links, such as donations of VR equipment or commercial contracts, are hard to disentangle. Nevertheless, I would estimate that the number of staff dedicated to VR research at these four laboratories for the period of 1991–1994 is between five and twenty-five, with annual spending on VR research in the range of $2 million to $50 million.

5. See Neugebauer (1993). There are, in fact, three related Fraunhofer Institutes in Stuttgart: the Institute for Building Physics, the Institute for Man-

ufacturing Engineering and Automation, and the Institute for Industrial Engineering. Another Fraunhofer Institute in Darmstadt has been mainly undertaking computer graphics research for VR. The VR group has links with all of these.

6. It should be noted that there have been many such VR showpiece demonstrations. So, for example, a well-publicized early application of VR has supposedly been in visualizing complex stock exchange information in 3-D (Aukstakalnis and Blatner 1992:240–242). This application received extensive media coverage and was described as if VR were already being used on an everyday basis. But although the idea of stock exchange analysts flying around in virtual financial markets is intriguing, in fact, this type of VR system has not been used, apart from demonstration purposes.

7. An overview of the socioeconomic approaches to the diffusion of new technologies can be found in Heimer (1994).

8. The Stuttgart institute has therefore recently shifted its efforts away from the use of VR in relation to robotics (Neugebauer 1992) to focus on the use of VR for factory planning and other visualization purposes (Neugebauer 1994, Segura 1994:31–32).

9. Interview with Tachi, September 21, 1994.

10. Following the demise of Lanier's VPL, the Bristol-based firm Division has become one of the foremost producers of commercially available VR systems.

11. The background of both labs is detailed by Rheingold (1991).

12. Another free software package is Minimal Reality from the University of Alberta (Kalawsky 1993:225–234). But neither VEOS nor Minimal Reality have become widely used. On the development of VEOS, see Bricken and Coco (1994).

13. "Blue and green laser diodes are not yet available, although they are expected to be available in 3 to 5 years" (Holmgren and Robinett 1993:183).

14. For the same reasons, the largest shared virtual world (to my knowledge) to date has been built by a military institution, the Naval Postgraduate School. More than ten postgraduate students have been working on this world since 1990, so that "what started as a simple system with a lone vehicle in a one kilometer square world, has now expanded to a fully networked system capable of supporting 500 vehicles of any of 2,000 types in a world exceeding 100 kilometers on a side"(Pratt et al. 1995:90).

15. Postmodern writers like Der Derian (1994) and Sterling (1993) think that computer simulations, including VR, make war more likely and more lethal, but there is no evidence to support their claims. Der Derian also suggests that military leaders should read French postmodern thinkers (1994:122), which seems improbable.

16. For Japan, see Watson (1994).

17. These figures are taken from *VR News,* vol. 4, issue no. 6, July 1995, p. 20 and derived from figures provided by John Latta of 4th Wave Inc. Latta's figures are the most widely cited estimates for VR markets. In 1995, he calculated that $49.1 million would be spent on VR R&D worldwide, $13.2 million for business and marketing uses of VR, and $190.3 million for public entertainment and consumer uses of VR. Total spending on VR, according to Latta, would be $257 million in 1995 (the shortfall to the total is made up by a $4.4 million catch-all "other" category). These figures are only estimates and they do not include government spending for VR. It can be estimated, however, that the bulk of government spending, apart from the money invested in networking facilities for military training simulations, goes toward buying VR equipment from commercial suppliers for the use of VR in military training (and, to a lesser extent, for use in other projects such as telesurgery). Even if we assume that government military spending is two or three times as much as Latta's total of $257 million for civilian spending (which is an estimate that several military and nonmilitary sources have suggested to me), military spending does not directly influence VR research, or VR systems, since the U.S. military mainly buys off-the-shelf commercial VR systems. One exception here may be that the U.S. military has purchased large numbers of HMDs with a higher resolution than most commercial systems, but high-resolution screens are being sought in civilian markets, too. In any case, the military uses of VR do not exercise a major influence on VR, given that military training is highly specialized. Instead, the main influence of the military, as we have seen, may be on standards for networked VR. And again, the applicability of these standards to networked entertainment games is currently being explored (Katz 1994).

18. Several of the government initiatives have already been mentioned, like the support of the European Community, the National Research Council study, and the efforts of the German and Japanese governments.

19. Interview with Slater, October 25, 1994.

20. The line between simulator games and VR games is hard to draw. Still, as VR-1 and Flying Aces use HMDs, they can be included here.

21. A counterexample might be the Virtuality game Flying Aces, in which a virtual copilot is generated in order to act as a kind of flying instructor. This feature makes considerable demands on the system's hardware and software. Whether it adds to the enjoyment of the game is another matter.

22. This happens to be the arrangement in Tachi's laboratory, although the user and the robot could be in completely separate locations, as long as there is an information link between them.

23. Interview with Tachi, September 21, 1994.

24. It should be noted that although there is obviously a great difference between using VR systems for gaining skills in the real world as opposed to

using them only to experience the virtual worlds themselves, from a sociological point of view, the latter is no less "real" in terms of its implications than the former, since both entail people spending time in virtual worlds, whether for leisure or for work.

25. It can be mentioned that Slater and his colleagues are not the only researchers investigating "presence." Steve Ellis, for example, has recently begun research that focuses not on "presence" as such, but on the measurement of task peformance in virtual environments and how the measurements provide insight into the experience of the user (Ellis, forthcoming).

26. In Chapter 6, we will encounter a number of cultural theorists who argue that the body entering cyberspace implies the breaking down of boundary between humans and machines or between reality and the simulation of reality. But the boundaries do not break down: VR systems produce computer-generated worlds via which users experience being in an environment other than the one in which they are physically present. Whether, if these machines are used for long periods, the experiences that users have of their real bodies or of the real world also change, which is suggested by the notion that various boundaries are breaking down, is a separate question that has not yet, to my knowledge, been investigated, except perhaps in science fiction.

Chapter 4

1. For some preliminary thoughts on this topic, see Bricken and Byrne (1992); Brown, Cobb, and Eastgate (1994); Schroeder, Cleal, and Giles (1993); Schroeder, Cleal, and Giles (1994); Schroeder (1995b).

2. The author's visit to the school took place in August 1992.

3. Further details can be found in Bricken and Byrne (1992); Byrne (1992); Bricken (1990).

4. For a brief description of this device, see Kalawsky (1993:207).

5. Giles spent eight weeks as a participant observer at the school between May and July 1992, and the author made two visits during the same period.

6. One interesting feature of the Dangerous Workplace world was that one of the forklift trucks got lost (i.e., it drove out of the factory space and could not be retrieved, although on occasion it would unexpectedly come driving back into the factory).

7. For the HITLab questionnaire results, see Bricken and Byrne (1992). Fifty-nine pupils participated in the HITLab questionnaire, most of them male. The West Denton questionnaire was given to thirty-five students who had used the VR systems and thirty-five who had not. Their average age was 14.25 years and just over 80 percent were male, with a slightly lower percentage (approximately 60 percent) of males among the non-VR users (see

Schroeder, Cleal, and Giles 1993, for further details). The results of these questionnaires can only serve to give some overall impressions, as the sample size, methodology, and limited experience with VR do not allow any systematic conclusions.

8. It can be noted that unlike the virtual worlds of science fiction writers such as William Gibson and Neal Stephenson, which emphasize dystopian features like violence, the worlds of the pupils at West Denton and the HITLab tended to envisage peaceful and optimistic scenarios; and unlike the virtual worlds of academic theorists like Stone and Haraway (they will be discussed in Chapter 6), which seek to remedy specific ills such as gender inequalities, the pupils' worlds were utopian in a more general sense.

9. This part of the chapter is based on the observations of Cleal (see also Schroeder, Cleal, and Giles 1994), who worked for ten weeks at the Shepherd School in Nottingham and with the Virtual Reality Applications Research Team (VIRART) at Nottingham University from June to August 1993. The author also visited VIRART during this period. At the Shepherd School, Cleal worked with twenty-five pupils over a two-week period while they were using the VR system.

10. The resources for this project came from Dimension, the Shepherd School, and a local brewery.

11. A more detailed discussion can be found in Schroeder, Cleal, and Giles (1994).

12. The software developed by VIRART has since become commercially available through a U.K. firm, Rompa, that specializes in products for people with learning difficulties. The products listed in the firm's 1994 sales brochure include four VIRART worlds—City World, Ski World, Supermarket Shopping World, and House World—that are "designed to enable people with severe and profound learning difficulties to experience both everyday situations and sporting and recreation activities." The brochure cites the experience at the Shepherd School to promote these products as tools for special needs learning. It is noteworthy that the brochure does not mention virtual reality, though it describes the hardware that is required (aside from a personal computer and spaceball or joystick) as a "simulator." There has been much interest in VR for special needs and disability applications (see, for example, the special issue of the journal *Presence—Teleoperators and Virtual Environments* 3:3 1994).

An important point that has been made by Ian Gwalter is that all, not just those with disabilities, seek to have enhanced abilities in the virtual world (for instance, wanting to fly) that they do not have in the real world (Wood and Gwalter 1995).

13. Stone (1993) makes a distinction between "creative" (i.e., building worlds) and "noncreative" VR.

14. At a conference presentation in London, April 1993.

15. The owner of a game arcade in Brisbane, Australia, which operated Waldern's machines, informed me in April 1993 that many players had purchased expensive life memberships at the arcade at a cost of over $150 (U.S.), which entitled them to play VR games at a reduced price. That they signed up *before* they had played their first game gives an indication of the enthusiasm that surrounded VR when it first became available to the public.

16. A similar phenomenon can be found in relation to computer games. See, for example, Haddon (1993).

17. The same thing happened to Dimension's desktop VR software. Initially called Superscape Alternate Realities, the software became known as virtual reality software in 1991 (interview with Ian Andrew, managing director of Dimension, now Superscape, July 16, 1992). Waldern's prototype machines were, incidentally, a "garage" effort, just like Lanier's (*Black Ice* 1993:15).

18. According to Dysart (1995:23), more than 700 Virtuality machines had been installed worldwide by 1995.

19. Players interviewed by Whittingdon (1992:33).

20. Interview with Warren Robinett, July 16, 1992.

21. Waldern at a conference presentation in London, April 5, 1993.

22. This is not to say that the two characteristics are mutually exclusive: A "virtual drum kit," for example, can also be played as part of an immersive VR system. Bob Stone, a prominent VR researcher in Britain, was interviewed playing an immersive virtual drum on the BBC Radio 4 program "One Step Beyond: Virtual Valerie" (broadcast on November 21, 1992) and declared himself delighted with the game.

23. For a classification of VR games by content, see Adam et al. (1993).

24. This trial was carried out by AT&T, the American telecommunications company (Tran 1993). The finding that networked games are among the most popular uses of interactive television has been reinforced by more recent trials (interview with Johnny Green of Time Warner Cable Full Service Network, August 13, 1995).

25. Mintel Leisure Intelligence, vol.1, 1992.

26. Peter Main of Nintendo quoted by Provenzo (1991:14).

27. Mintel Leisure Intelligence, vol. 1, 1992. Mackay (1995) argues, however, that there are significant socioeconomic differences in home computer ownership.

28. There are, however, various projects under way to explore the possibility of pay-per-play computer and VR games that are networked to the home.

29. It might be useful to present data about average duration of play here, but there are, to my knowledge, few sources for this. Parsons (1995) offers a review of studies of computer games, which have often focused on "addiction." This notion has also been the focus of research in psychology. Griffiths (1991), for example, reviews the debates in psychology about "addiction"

and more recent essays present some of the findings about the link between aggression and computer games (1993). In the context of psychological research, however, the most interesting notion may be what Griffiths calls "technological addiction," which he defines as "nonchemical (behavioral) addictions which involve human-machine interaction. They can be passive (e.g., television) or active (e.g., computer games) and usually contain inducing and reinforcing features which may contribute to the promotion of addictive tendencies" (1995:15).

30. A more complete list can be found in Kalawsky (1993:40).

31. See, for example, Biocca (1992a). Pausch, Crea, and Conway (1992) provide a review of the literature on simulator sickness.

32. Biocca (1992a:341); cf. Durlach and Mavor (1994:205–230). It is also possible that users may "adapt" to being in a virtual environment over time or that antimotion-sickness drugs may alleviate some of the side effects, but investigation of these areas is still at an early stage (Regan 1995:17–32).

33. A discussion of the concept of "moral panics," including an overview of recent research on this topic, can be found in Marshall (1990:149–175).

34. A good example of media coverage of health and safety issues that mixed concern and moral panic was a front page article in a British newspaper in response to the announcement of the imminent launch of a home VR game: "Sega game could cause eye damage" (Connor and Watts 1993:1). As it happens, the game was delayed, though not as a result of any specific media coverage. Nevertheless, while airing some well-founded concerns, the article was also an example of a "moral panic," inasmuch as it was not based on any evidence showing that specific home VR games could, in fact, cause eye damage.

35. Bob Stone, a prominent figure in VR research in Britain, predicted early on that "possibly even before the end of 1992, we will see the first domestic virtual reality system," adding "after that, I believe that's the end of civilization as we know it" (quoted by Glass 1992:20). This prediction was premature on both counts.

36. After reviewing the work on active audiences, Silverstone comes to the conclusion that "the notion of the active viewer can no longer be sustained" (1994:157–158).

37. The following passage, for example, seems to sum up the yearning for imaginary virtual worlds perfectly: "Modern hedonism presents all individuals with the possibility of being their own despot, exercising total control over the stimuli they experience, and hence the pleasure they receive" (Campbell 1987:76). Campbell goes on to explain that "this control is achieved through the power of imagination and provides infinitely greater possibilities for the maximization of pleasurable experiences than was available under traditional, realistic hedonism . . . it is this highly rationalized form of self-illusory hedo-

nism which characterizes modern pleasure-seeking" (1987:76; in relation to VR, see also Cleal 1994).

Chapter 5

1. This section is based on Schroeder (1995c).

2. For a brief description of the technical features of the VR system, see Kalawsky (1993:39–40).

3. An overview of the sociological analysis of "facework," derived from the work of Erving Goffman, can be found in Collins (1988:251–252 and passim).

4. An account of the principles of film narration can be found, for example, in Bordwell (1985:27–146). It is important to bear in mind that the principles underlying film narration and the workings of other artificial images should not necessarily be counterposed to everyday vision. Messaris, for example, has argued that the faculty of perceiving artificial images as realistic ones may be less of an acquired skill than is often thought (1994:13 and passim).

5. On the idea of mutual awareness in VR, see Benford and Fahlen (1992).

6. Some of the psychological aspects of "realism" in VR are discussed by Carr and England (1993).

7. Ellis (1995:41) makes a similar point in relation to VR systems that are used for professional or nonentertainment purposes.

8. There is little difference, incidentally, between an entertainment game flight simulator such as Kinney Aero's Fightertown and flight simulators used by the military for training jet pilots (I have "flown" an F–16 jet in entertainment and military settings). The main difference is that for military training, more realistic tasks will be set.

9. It is interesting to note that there is evidence to suggest that world-building may make a difference to the feeling of "presence" in the virtual world. A study of children at the HITLab "found that responses to 'Did you feel that were part of the virtual world?' were significantly and positively correlated with 'How much did you enjoy designing and building a virtual world?'" (Barfield et al. 1995:508–509).

10. This section is based on Schroeder (1994a).

11. One way to draw attention to the extent to which we take the visual environment for granted is by reference to the experience of blind or partially sighted people. This was brought home to me at an arts installation entitled Dialogue in the Dark (the installation was devised by Andreas Heinecke of the Stiftung Blindenanstalt, Frankfurt, and took place in London at the Royal Festival Hall, May 4 through June 18, 1995). The installation

consisted of a forty-five-minute tour of four environments in complete darkness: a park landscape, a street, a living room, and a bar. In experiencing these environments, I had to rely on my senses of touch and hearing (and to a lesser extent smell) more than I had ever done before. What this experience of a nonvisual world also made me aware of, however, was the disproportionate "load" that vision bears in our experience of everyday environments.

12. A noteworthy feature of virtual worlds (which also applies to simulators) is that virtual time can be speeded up. Thus it has been found that fighter pilots trained to perform certain tasks in VR with the virtual world running 1.6 times faster than real time are able to perform these tasks better than those trained in real time (Guckenberger 1995). It is not known whether these effects of speeded-up training apply to other tasks as well.

13. VR is evaluated in relation to other HCI tools by MacKenzie (1995).

14. See Morningstar and Farmer (1991). Habitat is an interesting example: Dr. Kazutomo Fukuda, manager of the Cyberspace Systems Development department of Fujitsu Ltd., which plans to relaunch the Habitat system, told me (interview September 22, 1994) that Habitat has more than 9,900 users in Japan, many of whom have spent long periods interacting with others in these 2-D graphical worlds. Fukuda has thus been able to observe some unexpected phenomena. For example, although 90 percent of the users of this system are male and 10 percent are female, in the Habitat world, 50 percent adopt male and 50 percent female identities (one of the most frequently visited places in the Habitat world is the sex-change clinic).

15. Artists were among the first to exploit VR as a medium of expression (Shaw 1991; Stenger 1992). Like other new media, VR has raised new aesthetic challenges. See, for example, Benedikt (1991), Heim (1993), and Laurel (1991). VR artworks, incidentally, often face the same problem as VR arcade entertainment games; namely, that only a single user can experience the work of art at one time with an HMD. This makes "throughput" difficult.

16. Steuer's comparison uses two separate dimensions for vividness and interactivity (1995). The disadvantage of such categorization, or of using three dimensions, as in Zeltzer's case (1992), is that no direct comparison can be made that puts VR on a single scale with other technologies. Steuer, incidentally, also classes VR as a "media technology," but he includes books and paintings under the label "medium," which makes the category very broad. For our purposes, as I shall argue in Chapter 7, it makes sense to restrict "medium" to an exchange of information.

17. For a discussion of some of the issues raised by the convergence of VR and communication technologies, drawing on Curtis's experience with MUDs (1992), see Schroeder (1995d).

Chapter 6

1. The use of cyborg does not necessarily correspond to the typical usage in science fiction, where the term refers to a wholly artificially created organism or being. Instead, this notion envisions some kind of fusion between humans and machines.

2. The first part of this chapter is based on Schroeder (1994b).

3. For their role in early VR development, see Rheingold (1991). Since withdrawing from VPL, Lanier has become a VR music performer. Laurel works at Interval Research, a recently founded VR start-up company.

4. Lanier cited by Woolley (1992:20).

5. Laurel in an interview with Jas Morgan (1992:84).

6. Although it is often hard to tell whether these theorists are concerned with VR and related technologies or with changes in the relation between humans and machines generally. Stone and Haraway seem to focus on the relation between humans and machines, while Kroker draws more directly on VR, characterizing "the age in which we live" as "the Age under the sign of the Will to Virtuality" and identifying VR as the "dream of liberal fascism" (Kroker interviewed by Sharon Grace, 1993:63). He asserts that "the dominant form of consciousness in the world today is television" and that he "view[s] television now as almost a preliminary phase in preparing the masses of humanity for virtual reality" (1993:64). Liberation is nevertheless possible: "I would say the most radical action is saying 'No' while saying 'Yes' to technology—or critically distancing yourself while drowning your body in high tech. Cruising the electronic frontier at hyperspeed with a copy of Nietzsche's *Will to Power* in your virtual hands"(1993:65). While Kroker's inspiration may be overtly Nietzschean, he also hints at the Feuerbachian roots of his thinking: "I do most of my writing at McDonald's"(1993:63).

7. All quotes refer to the author's visit on June 24, 1992.

8. The author's visits took place on August 4 and 5, 1992.

9. On a second visit to the Cyberseed Club in London on December 3, 1993, it was noticeable that the use of the prefix "cyber" had become more common: the "cyberfashion" show, for example, exhibited "cyberstyle."

10. Laurel interviewed by Morgan (1992:84).

11. (Haraway 1991:173). A selection of cyberpunk stories and commentaries on cyberpunk fiction can be found in the volume edited by Larry McCaffery (1991).

12. This is a variation on the title of William Gibson's science fiction novel *Neuromancer,* which makes use of VR-like technology.

13. For the importance of the consumption of ICTs in the home, see the essays in Silverstone and Hirsch (1992).

14. For a Durkheimian analysis of beliefs about the role of computers, see Alexander (1992).

15. I have focused on the early manifestations of cyberculture, but many more recent examples could be given. For example, the French thinker Jean Baudrillard, in a recent essay in the U.K. edition of *Wired* magazine, mentions "virtual reality" and "virtual" on fifteen occasions in an essay that is little more than a page long, suggesting, among other things, that "our own reality doesn't exist anymore" and announcing the "transformation of life itself into virtual reality" (1995:54). Darley has suggested in an article on computer graphics that the postmodern view of new information and communication technologies is that "culture *becomes* simulation" (1990:59). It is not clear to me what evidence could be used to support these statements, or, for example, for the following: "Postmodernists understand keenly how human identity itself is a virtual reality, as much a technological artifact as it is an expression of individual agency" (Balsamo 1995:366).

16. For more examples of the cultural phenomena surrounding VR, see Woolley (1992).

17. The advertisement appeared, for example, in *The Guardian* newspaper on April 16, 1993, on p. 2.

Chapter 7

1. Robins and Webster (1989) have made a similar point in relation to the use of microcomputers in the classroom.

2. A further and more general factor that has a strong bearing on VR in education is the interest of large telecommunications companies in fostering educational applications of networked VR. But since these schemes are still in their infancy, it is impossible to make conjectures about their possible influence.

3. Winner (1986) makes this argument about computers; see also Mackay (1995) in relation to information technology in the home.

4. Hughes has recently made use of the notion of "technological momentum" to make the point that "a technological system . . . can shape or be shaped by society. As they grow larger and more complex, systems tend to be more shaping of society and less shaped by it . . . the social constructivists have a key to understanding the behavior of young systems; technical determinists come into their own with the mature ones" (1994:112). For this reason, he says, "the momentum of technological systems is a concept that can be located somewhere between the poles of technical determinism and social constructivism" (1994:112). It will be interesting to see whether this also applies over the longer term to a stand-alone technology like VR—as opposed to the "large technological systems" that Hughes is describing. As

we have seen, however, in the case of VR, a "young" technology can also shape social life as well as shaped by it.

5. The most widely cited example of VR systems being used to save costs has been in the automotive industry, where testing VR models of vehicles has to some extent been substituted for building and modifying expensive prototypes.

6. Ellis (1991:326). Several writers share Ellis's view that VR is a communications technology or a medium (Biocca 1992a; Steuer 1995; Biocca and Levy 1995).

7. Degele points out that the confusion over whether computers are communication tools arises from the fact that "no clear distinction is made between communication 'with' and 'through' computers" (1994:231). It seems to me, however, that the idea of communication "through" (single-user) computers can only be posed at an abstract level of their function in society as a whole. A functionalist argument along these lines has been put forward by Esposito (1993).

8. The idea that "all computer-based interactivity is a form of interaction with other humans, even when none are present" since "the human presence of the programmers and designers remains resident in the *logic and structure* of the artificial interaction" (Biocca and Levy 1995:146) would apply to so many objects in our everyday life as to make the notion of interaction meaningless.

9. Biocca (1992b:14), where he cites Kubey and Csikszentmihalyi (1990:xi).

10. A similar point has been made by Bill Gates, president of the software company Microsoft (quoted by Haynes 1994:22). A good discussion of how the personal computer fits into the home is provided by Haddon (1992).

11. Jaron Lanier, Thomas Furness III, director of the HITLab, and Frederick Brooks of the University of North Carolina at Chapel Hill were among the expert witnesses.

12. The relation between innovation and economic advantage with respect to the rivalry between the United States and Japan is in fact more complex than this mythical image implies. See, for example, Inkster (1991). The same applies to Gore's political analysis: In an article concerning the information superhighway, Gore likened distributed computer networks to the positive aspects of capitalism and presented communism as a "large and powerful central processor, which collapsed when it was overwhelmed by ever more complex information" (1991:108).

13. This is the first complete VR *system* for domestic entertainment. Several inexpensive HMDs and 3-D joysticks for gaming are already on the market.

14. Garton and Wellman (1995) provide a recent overview of some of the research on the effects of computer-mediated communication.

15. The technology for "garage" or amateur VR is catalogued and explained by Hollands (1996). Another path that could put VR in the hands of a much wider public and thus transform it is the Internet. This transformation has recently begun with VRML, which allows users to import a 3-D world and world-building capabilities. So far, however, VRML is confined to "desktop" VR and supports a limited degree of interaction.

16. It is also possible that professional VR systems are used for longer periods: In a recent lecture, Frederick Brooks mentioned that the longest he had ever seen anyone inside a virtual environment was when a Polish research scientist visited the UNC lab and became so involved in trying to dock "molecules" together that he spent two-and-a-half hours "inside" (1994).

17. In Hitchener's (1995) overview of some of the most commonly used commercial VR software, for example, seven out of sixteen software products supported world design. Of these, five supported world design on the desktop computer and two from within the virtual world (or "immersively"). In this context, it is worth mentioning again that the first commercial VR systems produced by VPL featured immersive world-building.

18. For a related argument about how microelectronics technologies have flattened organizational hierarchies and transformed economic activity, see Dudley (1991:267–309).

References

Adam, John A. 1993. "Virtual Reality is for Real." *IEEE Spectrum*, October, pp. 22–28.

Adam, Pascal, et al. 1993. "Systemes Ludiques et Realites Virtuelles." In *Interface to Real and Virtual Worlds*. Paris: EC2, pp. 287–292.

Agassi, Joseph. 1985. *Technology, Philosophical and Social Aspects*. Dordrecht: D. Reidel.

Alexander, Jeffrey. 1992. "The Promise of a Cultural Sociology: Technological Discourse and the Sacred and Profane Information Machine." In Richard Münch and Neil Smelser (Eds.), *Theory of Culture*. Berkeley: University of California Press, pp. 293–323.

Argyle, Michael. 1992. *The Social Psychology of Everyday Life*. London: Routledge.

Astheimer, Peter, et al. 1994. "Industrielle Anwendungen der Virtuellen Realität—Beispiele, Erfahrungen, Probleme und Zukunftsperspektiven." In H.-J. Warnecke and H.-J. Bullinger (Eds.), *Virtual Reality '94—Anwendungen und Trends*. Berlin: Springer, pp. 259–280.

Aukstakalnis, Steve, and David Blatner. 1992. *Silicon Mirage: The Art and Science of Virtual Reality*. Berkeley: Peachpit Press.

Auzenne, Valliere Richard. 1994. *The Visualization Quest: A History of Computer Animation*. Rutherford, N.J.: Fairleigh Dickinson University Press.

Bajura, Michael, Henry Fuchs, and Ryutarou Ohbuchi. 1992. "Merging Virtual Objects with the Real World: Seeing Ultrasound Imagery Within the Patient." *Computer Graphics* 26 (2):203–210.

Balsamo, Anne. 1995. "Signal to Noise: On the Meaning of Cyberpunk Subculture." In Frank Biocca and Mark Levy (Eds.), *Communication in the Age of Virtual Reality*. Hillsdale, N.J.: Lawrence Erlbaum Associates, pp. 347–368.

Barfield, Woodrow, and Thomas Furness III (Eds.). 1995. *Virtual Environments and Advanced Interface Design*. Oxford: Oxford University Press.

Barfield, Woodrow, et al. 1995. "Presence and Performance within Virtual Environments." In Woodrow Barfield and Thomas Furness III (Eds.), *Virtual Environments and Advanced Interface Design*. Oxford: Oxford University Press, pp. 473–513.

Barfield, Woodrow, Craig Rosenberg, and Wouter A. Lotens. 1995. "Augmented-Reality Displays." In Woodrow Barfield and Thomas Furness III

(Eds.), *Virtual Environments and Advanced Interface Design*. Oxford: Oxford University Press, pp. 542–575.

Bartle, Richard. 1990. "Interactive Multiuser Computer Games." *MUSE Ltd.* (Unpublished research report), December.

Baudrillard, Jean. 1995. "The Perfect Crime." *Wired* (U.K. edition) 1(2):54–55.

Bell, Daniel. 1979. "The Social Framework of the Information Society." In Michael Dertouzos and Joel Moses (Eds.), *The Computer Age: A Twenty-Year View*. Cambridge, Mass.: MIT Press, pp. 163–211.

Benedikt, Michael (Ed.). 1991. *Cyberspace: First Steps*. Cambridge, Mass.: MIT Press.

Benford, Stephen. 1994. "The Virtuosi Project." In Sandra Helsel (Ed.), *Proceedings of the Fourth Annual Conference on Virtual Reality*. London: Meckler, pp. 131–139.

Benford, Stephen, and Lennart Fahlen. 1992. "Aura, Focus, and Awareness." In Lennart Fahlen and Kai-Mikael Jää-Aro (Eds.), *Proceedings of the Fifth MultiG Workshop*. Stockholm: Royal Institute of Technology (no pp.).

Beniger, James. 1986. *The Control Revolution: Technological and Economic Origins of the Information Society*. Cambridge, Mass.: Harvard University Press.

Bijker, Wiebe, Thomas Hughes, and Trevor Pinch (Eds.). 1987. *The Social Construction of Technological Systems*. Cambridge, Mass.: MIT Press.

Biocca, Frank. 1992a. "Communication Within Virtual Reality: Creating a Space for Research." *Journal of Communication* 42 (2):5–22.

Biocca, Frank. 1992b. "Will Simulation Sickness Slow Down the Diffusion of Virtual Environment Technology." *Presence: Teleoperators and Virtual Environments* 1(3):334–345.

Biocca, Frank, and Ben Delaney. 1995. "Immersive Virtual Reality Technology." In Frank Biocca and Mark Levy (Eds.), *Communication in the Age of Virtual Reality*. Hillsdale, N.J.: Lawrence Erlbaum Associates, pp. 57–124.

Biocca, Frank, and Mark Levy. 1995. "Communication Applications of Virtual Reality." In Frank Biocca and Mark Levy (Eds.), *Communication in the Age of Virtual Reality*. Hillsdale, N.J.: Lawrence Erlbaum Associates, pp. 127–157.

Biocca, Frank, Taeyong Kim, and Mark Levy. 1995. "The Vision of Virtual Reality." In Frank Biocca and Mark Levy (Eds.), *Communication in the Age of Virtual Reality*. Hillsdale, N.J.: Lawrence Erlbaum Associates, pp. 3–14.

Bishop, Katherine. 1992. "The Electronic Coffeehouse." *New York Times*, August 2, p. 21.

Black Ice. 1993. "W Industries." 1, January, pp. 12–19, 54–57.

Bordwell, David. 1985. *Narration in the Fiction Film*. London: Methuen.

Brand, Stewart. 1987. *The Media Lab: Inventing the Future at MIT*. New York: Viking Penguin.

Bricken, Meredith. 1990. "A Description of the Virtual Reality Learning Environment." *Human Interface Technology Laboratory Technical Report*, HITL-M-90-4.

Bricken, Meredith. 1991. "Gender Issues in Virtual Reality Technology." *Human Interface Technology Laboratory Technical Publication*, HITL-P-91-6.

Bricken, Meredith, and Chris Byrne. 1992. "Summer Students in Virtual Reality: A Pilot Study on Educational Applications of Virtual Reality Technology." (Unpublished paper).

Bricken, William, and Geoff Coco. 1994. "The VEOS Project." *Presence: Teleoperators and Virtual Environments* 3(2):111–129.

Brooks, Frederick. 1988. "Grasping Reality Through Illusion." *Proceedings of CHI'88*. Reading, Mass.: Addison Wesley, pp. 1–11.

Brooks, Frederick, et al. 1990. "Project GROPE—Haptic Displays for Scientific Visualization." *Computer Graphics* 24(4):177–185.

Brooks, Frederick. 1994. "Is There Any Real Virtue in Virtual Reality?" Paper presented at the Institution of Electrical Engineers, London, November 30.

Brown, David. 1993. "Virtual Reality, Virtually Unlimited." *British Journal of Special Education* 20(1):12.

Brown, David, Sue Cobb, and Richard Eastgate. 1994. "Living in Virtual Environments (LIVE)." In Huw Jones, John Vince, and Rae Earnshaw (Eds.), *Virtual Reality Applications*, Proceedings of the British Computer Society Displays Group Conference, Leeds (no pp.).

Brubaker, Rogers. 1984. *The Limits of Rationality: An Essay on the Social and Moral Thought of Max Weber*. London: George Allen and Unwin.

Bruckman, Amy, and Mitchell Resnick. 1995. "The MediaMOO Project: Constructionism and Professional Community." *Convergence: The Journal of Research into New Media Technologies* 1(1):94–109.

Buckert-Donelson, Angela. 1995. "VR People: Dean Inman." *VR World* 3(1):23–26.

Burdea, Grigore, and Philip Coiffet. 1994. *Virtual Reality Technology*. New York: John Wiley and Sons.

Byrne, Chris. 1992. "Students Explore VR Technology." *HITLab Review*, 1, Winter, pp. 6–7.

Campbell, Colin. 1987. *The Romantic Ethic and the Spirit of Modern Consumerism*. Oxford: Basil Blackwell.

Carr, Karen, and Rupert England. 1993. "The Role of Realism in Virtual Reality." In Tony Feldman (Ed.), *VR93—Proceedings of the Third Annual Conference on Virtual Reality*. London: Meckler, pp. 24–33.

Cawson, Alan, Leslie Haddon, and Ian Miles. 1995. *The Shape of Things to Consume: Delivering Information Technology into the Home*. Aldershot: Avebury.

City of Newcastle-upon-Tyne Education Department. 1991. "Educational Achievement 16–19, Examination Performance in Newcastle Schools." (Unpublished report).

Clark, Michael. 1992. "Virtual Reality in Education and Training—Willing Prisoner of Its Own Flawed Metaphor." Paper presented at *VR92—The Second Annual Conference on Virtual Reality*, London.

Cleal, Bryan. 1994. "Virtual Reality—The Process of Innovation." B.Sc. dissertation, Department of Human Sciences, Brunel University.

Collins, Randall. 1986. *Weberian Sociological Theory*. Cambridge: Cambridge University Press.

Collins, Randall. 1988. *Theoretical Sociology*. New York: Harcourt Brace Jovanovich.

Collins, Randall. 1992. "On the Sociology of Intellectual Stagnation: The Late Twentieth Century in Perspective." *Theory, Culture and Society* 9: pp. 73–96.

Collins, Randall. 1994. "Why the Social Sciences Won't Become High-Consensus, Rapid-Discovery Science." *Sociological Forum* 9(2):155–177.

Collins, Randall, and Sal Restivo. 1983. "Development, Diversity and Conflict in the Sociology of Science." *Sociological Quarterly* 24:185–200.

Connor, Steve, and Susan Watts. 1993. "Sega Game Could Cause Eye Damage." *The Independent*, September 5, p. 1.

Cruz-Neira, Carolina, Daniel Sandin, and Thomas DeFanti. 1993. "Surround-Screen Projection-Based Virtual Reality: The Design and Implementation of the CAVE." *Computer Graphics Proceedings, Annual Conference Series*, pp. 135–142.

Curtis, Pavel. 1992. "Mudding: Social Phenomena in Text-Based Virtual Realities." Palo Alto: Xerox PARC (Unpublished report).

Darley, Andy. 1990. "From Abstraction to Simulation: Notes on the History of Computer Imaging." In Philip Hayward (Ed.), *Culture, Technology and Creativity*. London: John Libbey/Arts Council, pp. 39–64.

Degele, Nina. 1994. *Der Überfordete Computer: Zur Soziologie Menschlicher und Künstlicher Intelligenz*. Frankfurt am Main: Campus Verlag.

Der Derian, James. 1994. "Cyber-Deterrence." *Wired* 2(9):116–122 and 158.

Dierkes, Meinolf, and Ute Hoffmann (Eds.). 1992. *New Technology at the Outset: Social Forces in the Shaping of Technological Innovations*. Frankfurt am Main: Campus Verlag.

Downey, Gary Lee. 1992. "Human Agency in CAD/CAM technology." *Anthropology Today* 8(5):2–6.

Dudley, Leonard. 1991. *The Word and the Sword—How Techniques of Information and Violence Have Shaped our World*. Oxford: Blackwell.

Durlach, Nathaniel, and Anne Mavor. 1995. *Virtual Reality: Scientific and Technological Challenges.* Washington, D.C.: National Academy Press.

Dysart, Joe. 1995. "Not Just Kid Stuff Anymore." *VR World* 3(3):22–23.

Edwards, Paul. 1994. "From 'Impact' to Social Process: Computers in Society and Culture." In Sheila Jasanoff et al. (Eds.), *Handbook of Science and Technology Studies.* London: Sage, pp. 257–285.

Ellis, S.R. 1991. "Nature and Origins of Virtual Environments: A Bibliographical Essay." *Computing Systems in Engineering* 2(4):321–347.

Ellis, Stephen. 1995. "Virtual Environments and Environmental Instruments." In Karen Carr and Rupert England (Eds.), *Simulated and Virtual Realities.* London: Taylor and Francis, pp. 11–51.

Ellis, Stephen. Forthcoming. "Presence of Mind...." *Presence: Teleoperators and Virtual Environments.*

Elmer-Dewitt, Philip. 1993. "Cyberpunk!" *Time* (U.S. edition) 141(6), February 8, pp. 58–62.

Escobar, Arturo. 1994. "Welcome to Cyberia—Notes on the Anthropology of Cyberculture." *Current Anthropology* 35(3):211–231.

Esposito, Elena. 1993. "Der Computer als Medium und Maschine." *Zeitschrift für Soziologie* 22(5):338–354.

Feyerabend, Paul. 1978. *Science in a Free Society.* London: New Left Books.

Foley, James, and Andries Van Dam. 1982. *Fundamentals of Interactive Computer Graphics.* Reading, Mass.: Addison Wesley.

Freeman, Christopher. 1987. "The Case for Technological Determinism." In Ruth Finnegan, Graeme Salaman, and Kenneth Thompson (Eds.), *Information Technology: Social Issues.* Sevenoaks: Hodder and Stoughton, pp. 5–18.

Friedman, Andrew. 1989. *Computer Systems Development: History, Organization and Implementation.* Chichester: John Wiley and Sons.

Fox, Barry. 1993. "Here Is The (Virtual) Nine O'clock News. . . ." *New Scientist*, April 3, p. 22.

Garland, Roy (Ed.). 1982. *Microcomputers and Children in the Primary School.* Brighton: Falmer Press.

Garton, Laura, and Barry Wellman. 1995. "The Social Impacts of Electronic Mail in Organizations: A Review of the Research Literature." In Brant Burleson (Ed.), *Communication Yearbook*, vol. 18. London: Sage, pp. 434–453.

Gay, Eben. 1994. "Virtual Reality at the Natrona County School System: Building Virtual Worlds on a School Budget." *Virtual Reality World* 2(6):44–47.

Gifford, Don. 1991. *The Farther Shore: A Natural History of Perception.* New York: Vintage Books.

Giles, Warren. 1994. "The Virtual Divide: Conception and Consumption of Virtual Reality Entertainment." B.Sc. dissertation, Department of Human Sciences, Brunel University.

Glass, Frankie. 1992. *Theme Park Heaven*. London: Channel Four Television.

Gore, Al. 1991. "Infrastructure for the Global Village." *Scientific American*, September, pp. 108–111.

Grace, Sharon. 1993. "Codes of Privilege: Arthur Kroker." *Mondo 2000*, 11, pp. 60–67.

Griffiths, Mark. 1991. "Amusement Machine Playing in Childhood and Adolescence: A Comparative Analysis of Video Games and Fruit Machines." *Journal of Adolescence* 14:53–73.

Griffiths, Mark. 1993. "Are Computer Games Bad for Children?" *The Psychologist* 6:401–407.

Griffiths, Mark. 1995. "Technological Addictions." *Clinical Psychology Forum* 76:14–19.

Guckenberger, R. J. 1995. "Human Time Adaptability in Virtual Reality." Paper presented to the Royal Society conference on Virtual Reality in Society, Engineering and Science, London.

Hacking, Jan. 1983. *Representing and Intervening*. Cambridge: Cambridge University Press.

Haddon, Leslie. 1992. "Explaining ICT Consumption: The Case of the Home Computer." In Roger Silverstone and Eric Hirsch (Eds.), *Consuming Technologies: Media and Information in Domestic Spaces*. London: Routledge, pp. 82–96.

Haddon, Leslie. 1993. "Interactive Games." In Philip Hayward and Tana Wollen (Eds.), *Future Visions—New Technologies of the Screen*. London: British Film Institute, pp. 123–147.

Halbach, Wulf. 1994. *Interfaces: Medien- und Kommunikations Theoretische Elemente Einer Interface Theorie*. Munich: Wilhelm Fink Verlag.

Hann, Mike, and Rob Hubbard. 1993. "Molecular Visualization in Pharmaceutical Research." In Tony Feldman (Ed.), *VR93—Proceedings of the Third Annual Conference on Virtual Reality*. London: Meckler, pp. 122–125.

Haraway, Donna. 1991. "A Cyborg Manifesto: Science, Technology, and Socialist Feminism in the Late Twentieth Century." In her *Simians, Cyborgs and Women*. London: Free Association Books, pp. 149–181.

Haraway, Donna. 1992. "The Promises of Monsters: A Regenerative Politics for Inappropriate/d Others." In Lawrence Grossberg, Cary Nelson, and Paula Treichler (Eds.), *Cultural Studies*. London: Routledge, pp. 295–337.

Hard, Michael. 1994. *Machines Are Frozen Spirit: The Scientification of Refrigeration and Brewing in the 19th Century—A Weberian Interpretation*. Frankfurt am Main: Campus Verlag.

Harriss, Philip, and Campbell McKellar. 1992. "Realtime Lighting for Virtual Worlds." In Tony Feldman (Ed.), *VR92—Proceedings of the Second Annual Conference on Virtual Reality*. London: Meckler, pp. 37–43.

Haynes, Peter. 1994. "Survey: The Computer Industry." *The Economist*, September 17, supplement pp. 1–26.

Heeter, Carrie. 1992. "*Being* There: The Subjective Experience of Presence." *Presence: Teleoperators and Virtual Environments* 1(2):262–271.

Heilig, Morton Leonard. 1992 (originally published 1955). "El Cine del Futuro: The Cinema of the Future." *Presence: Teleoperators and Virtual Environments* 1(3):279–294.

Heim, Mike. 1993. *The Metaphysics of Virtual Reality.* New York: Oxford University Press.

Heimer, Thomas. 1994. *Zur Ökonomik der Entstehung von Technologien: Eine Theoretische und Empirische Erörterung am Beispiel des Intelligent Home.* Marburg: Metropolis.

Helsel, Sandra, and Susan DeNoble Doherty. 1992. *Virtual Reality Marketplace 1993.* London: Meckler.

Hitchener, Lew. 1995. "VR Software Development." *VR News* 4(4):26–29.

Hollands, Robin. 1996. *The Virtual Reality Homebrewer's Handbook.* New York: John Wiley and Sons.

Holmgren, Douglas, and Warren Robinett. 1993. "Scanned Laser Displays for Virtual Reality: A Feasibility Study." *Presence: Teleoperators and Virtual Environments* 2(3):171–184.

Hughes, Thomas. 1987. "The Evolution of Large Technological Systems." In Wiebe Bijker, Thomas Hughes, and Trevor Pinch (Eds.), *The Social Construction of Technological Systems.* Cambridge, Mass.: MIT Press, pp. 51–82.

Hughes, Thomas. 1989. *American Genesis—A Century of Invention and Technological Enthusiasm.* New York: Viking Penguin.

Hughes, Thomas. 1994. "Technological Momentum." In Merrit Roe Smith and Leo Marx (Eds.), *Does Technology Drive History? The Dilemma of Technological Determinism.* Cambridge, Mass.: MIT Press, pp. 101–113.

Inkster, Ian. 1991. "Made in America but Lost to Japan: Science, Technology, and Economic Performance in the Two Capitalist Superpowers." *Social Studies of Science* 21(1):157–178.

Jacob, Robert. 1995. "Eye Tracking in Advanced Interface Design." In Woodrow Barfield and Thomas Furness III (Eds.), *Virtual Environments and Advanced Interface Design.* Oxford: Oxford University Press, pp. 258–288.

Jones, Ann. 1995. "Constructivist Learning Theories and IT." In Nick Heap et al. (Eds.), *Information Technology and Society.* London: Sage, pp. 249–265.

Kalawsky, Roy. 1993. *The Science of Virtual Reality and Virtual Environments.* Reading, Mass.: Addison Wesley.

Katz, Warren. 1994. "Military Networking Technology Applied to Location-Based, Theme Park, and Home Entertainment Systems." *Computer Graphics* 28(2):110–112.

Kay, Helen. 1993. "Mayfair Enters Electronic Age." *The Independent on Sunday*, June 12 (Business), p. 6.

Krueger, Myron. 1991. *Artificial Reality II*. Reading, Mass.: Addison Wesley.

Kubey, Robert, and Mihaly Csikszentmihalyi. 1990. *Television and the Quality of Everyday Life*. Hillsdale, N.J.: Lawrence Erlbaum Associates.

Lampton, Donald, et al. 1994. "The Virtual Environment Performance Assessment Battery (VEPAB): Development and Evaluation." *Presence: Teleoperators and Virtual Environments* 3(2):145–157.

Lanier, Jaron. 1989. "Virtual Environments and Interactivity: Windows to the Future." *Computer Graphics* 23(5):8–9.

Lanier, Jaron, and Frank Biocca. 1992. "An Insider's View of the Future of Virtual Reality." *Journal of Communication* 42(2):150–172.

Latour, Bruno. 1993. *We Have Never Been Modern*. Hemel Hempstead: Harvester Wheatsheaf.

Laurel, Brenda. 1991. *Computers as Theatre*. Reading, Mass.: Addison-Wesley.

Levy, Steven. 1984. *Hackers: Heroes of the Computer Revolution*. New York: Doubleday.

MacCaffery, Larry (Ed.). 1991. *Storming the Reality Studio: A Casebook of Cyberpunk and Postmodern Science Fiction*. Durham, N.C.: Duke University Press.

Macedonia, Michael, et al. 1994. "NPSNET: A Network Software Architecture for Large-Scale Virtual Environments." *Presence: Teleoperators and Virtual Environments* 3(4):265–287.

Mackay, Hughie. 1995. "Patterns of Ownership of IT Devices in the Home." In Nick Heap et al. (Eds.), *Information Technology and Society*. London: Sage, pp. 311–340.

MacKenzie, Donald. 1991. "The Influence of the Los Alamos and Livermore National Laboratories on the Development of Supercomputing." *Annals of the History of Computing* 13(2):179–201.

MacKenzie, Donald, and Judy Wajcman (Eds.). 1985. *The Social Shaping of Technology*. Milton Keynes: Open University Press.

MacKenzie, I. Scott. 1995. "Input Devices and Interaction Techniques for Advanced Computing." In Woodrow Barfield and Thomas Furness III (Eds.), *Virtual Environments and Advanced Interface Design*. Oxford: Oxford University Press, pp. 437–470.

Marshall, Gordon. 1990. *In Praise of Sociology*. London: Unwin Hyman.

The Marxist. 1994. "Video Games and Virtual Reality." March, 51, pp. 20–24.

McLuhan, Marshall. 1964. *Understanding Media: The Extensions of Man*. New York: McGraw-Hill.

Messaris, Paul. 1994. *Visual "Literacy": Mind, Image, and Reality*. Boulder: Westview Press.

Meyer, Kenneth, Hugh Applewhite, and Frank Biocca. 1992. "A Survey of Position Trackers." *Presence: Teleoperators and Virtual Environments* 1(2):173–200.

Meyrowitz, Joshua. 1985. *No Sense of Place: The Impact of Electronic Media on Social Behaviour*. Oxford: Oxford University Press.

Mokyr, Joel. 1990. *The Lever of Riches—Technological Creativity and Economic Progress*. Oxford: Oxford University Press.

Molina, Alfonso Hernan. 1989. *The Social Basis of the Microelectronics Revolution*. Edinburgh: Edinburgh University Press.

Monaco, James. 1981. *How to Read a Film*. Oxford: Oxford University Press.

Morgan, Jas. 1992. "Brenda Laurel the Lizard Queen." *Mondo 2000*, 7, pp. 82–89.

Morningstar, Chip, and Randall Farmer. 1991. "The Lessons of Lucasfilm's Habitat." In Michael Benedikt (Ed.), *Cyberspace: First Steps*. Cambridge, Mass.: MIT Press, pp. 273–301.

Moshell, Michael, et al. 1995. "Research in Virtual Environments and Simulation at the Institute for Simulation and Training at the University of Central Florida." *Presence: Teleoperators and Virtual Environments* 4(2):209–217.

Neugebauer, Jens. 1992. "Industrial Applications of Virtual Reality: Robot Application Planning." In Tony Feldman (Ed.), *VR92—Proceedings of the Second Annual Conference on Virtual Reality*. London: Meckler, pp. 92–102.

Neugebauer, Jens. 1993. "Virtual Reality—The Demonstration Centre." In Tony Feldman (Ed.), *VR93—Proceedings of the Third Annual Conference on Virtual Reality*. London: Meckler, pp. 72–77.

Neugebauer, Jens. 1994. "Virtual Reality for the Pharmacy Industry." In Sandra Helsel (Ed.), *Proceedings of the Fourth Annual Conference on Virtual Reality*. London: Meckler, pp. 51–55.

Neumann, W. Russell. 1991. *The Future of the Mass Audience*. Cambridge: Cambridge University Press.

Noll, Michael. 1972. "Man-Machine Tactile Communication." *Journal of the Society for Information Display*, July/August 1972, pp. 6–11, 30.

Oman, Charles. 1991. "Sensory Conflict in Motion Sickness: An Observer Theory Approach." In Stephen Ellis (Ed.), *Pictorial Communication in Virtual and Real Environments*. London: Taylor and Francis, pp. 362–377.

Palfreman, Jon, and Doron Swade. 1991. *The Dream Machine: Exploring the Computer Age*. London: BBC Books.

Palmer, Mark. 1995. "Interpersonal Communication and Virtual Reality." In Frank Biocca and Mark Levy (Eds.), *Communication in the Age of Virtual Reality*. Hillsdale, N.J.: Lawrence Erlbaum Associates, pp. 277–299.

Parsons, Ken. 1995. "Educational Places or Terminal Cases: Young People and the Attraction of Computer Games." Paper presented to the British Sociological Association Annual Conference, *Social Change and the City*, Leicester.

Pausch, Randy, Thomas Crea, and Matthew Conway. 1992. "A Literature Survey for Virtual Environments: Military Flight Simulator Visual Systems and Simulator Sickness." *Presence: Teleoperators and Virtual Environments* 1(3):344–363.

Pfaffenberger, Bryan. 1992. "Social Anthropology of Technology." *Annual Review of Anthropology* 21, pp. 491–516.

Pratt, David, et al. 1995. "NPSNET: Four User Interface Paradigms for Entity Control in a Virtual World." *Journal of Intelligent Systems* 5(2–4):89–109.

Price, Derek de Solla. 1975. *Science Since Babylon* (second edition). New Haven: Yale University Press.

Provenzo, Eugene. 1991. *Video Kids: Making Sense of Nintendo*. Cambridge, Mass.: Harvard University Press.

Rammert, Werner. 1992. "Research on the Generation and Development of Technology: The State of the Art in Germany." In Meinolf Dierkes and Ute Hoffmann (Eds.), *New Technology at the Outset: Social Forces in the Shaping of Technological Innovations*. Frankfurt am Main: Campus Verlag, pp. 62–89.

Regan, Clare. 1995. "An Investigation into Nausea and Other Side-Effects of Head-Coupled Immersive Virtual Reality." *Virtual Reality* 1(1):17–32.

Restivo, Sal. 1994. "The Theory Landscape in Science Studies: Sociological Traditions." In Sheila Jassanoff et al. (Eds.), *Handbook of Science and Technology Studies*. London: Sage, pp. 95–110.

Rheingold, Howard. 1991. *Virtual Reality*. London: Secker and Warburg.

Rheingold, Howard. 1994. *The Virtual Community: Homesteading on the Electronic Frontier*. Reading, Mass.: Addison Wesley.

Robinett, Warren. 1992. "Synthetic Experience: A Proposed Taxonomy." *Presence: Teleoperators and Virtual Environments* 1(2):229–247.

Robins, Kevin, and Frank Webster. 1989. *The Technical Fix: Education, Computers, and Industry*. Basingstoke: Macmillan.

Rogers, Everett. 1986. *Communication Technology: The New Media in Society*. New York: Free Press.

Rushton, Simon, and John Wann. 1993. "Problems in Perception and Action in Virtual Worlds." In Tony Feldman (Ed.), *VR93—Proceedings of the Third Annual Conference on Virtual Reality*. London: Meckler, pp. 43–55.

Satava, Richard. 1994. "Update on Virtual Reality in Health Care: The New Future for Medicine and Surgery." In Sandra Helsel (Ed.), *Proceed-*

ings of the Fourth Annual Conference on Virtual Reality, London: Meckler, pp. 174–180.

Schroeder, Ralph. 1993. "Virtual Reality in the Real World: History, Applications, Projections." *Futures: A Journal of Forecasting, Planning and Policy* 25(9):963–973.

Schroeder, Ralph. 1994a. "Inside the Worlds of Cyberspace: A Sociological Typology of Virtual Realities." In Huw Jones, John Vince, and Rae Earnshaw (Eds.), *Virtual Reality Applications,* Proceedings of the British Computer Society Displays Group Conference, Leeds (no pp.).

Schroeder, Ralph. 1994b. "Cyberculture, Cyborg Postmodernism, and the Sociology of Virtual Reality Technologies: Surfing the Soul in the Information Age." *Futures: A Journal of Forecasting, Planning, and Policy* 26(5):519–528.

Schroeder, Ralph. 1995a. "Disenchantment and Its Discontents: Weberian Perspectives on Science and Technology." *Sociological Review* 43(3):227–250.

Schroeder, Ralph. 1995b. "Learning from Virtual Reality Applications in Education." *Virtual Reality* 1(1):33–40.

Schroeder, Ralph. 1995c. "Virtual Environments and the Varieties of Interactive Experience in Information and Communication Technologies." *Convergence: The Journal of Research into New Media Technologies* 1(2):45–55.

Schroeder, Ralph. 1995d. "Virtual Environments and the Future of Human-Computer Interfaces: The Electronic Frontier in Social Context." *Journal of Intelligent Systems* 5(2–4):111–123.

Schroeder, Ralph, Bryan Cleal, and Warren Giles. 1993. "Virtual Reality in Education: Some Preliminary Social Science Perspectives." *Interface to Real and Virtual Worlds.* Paris: EC2, pp. 147–158.

Schroeder, Ralph, Bryan Cleal, and Warren Giles. 1994. "Virtual Reality im Sprachunterricht für Lernbehinderte." In H.-J. Warnecke and H.-J. Bullinger (Eds.), *Virtual Reality '94: Anwendungen und Trends.* Berlin: Springer, pp. 227–240.

Schroeder, Ralph, Warren Giles, and Bryan Cleal. 1994. "Virtual Reality and the Future of Interactive Games." In H.-J. Warnecke and H.-J. Bullinger (Eds.), *Virtual Reality '94: Anwendungen und Trends.* Berlin: Springer, pp. 377–391.

Segura, Jean. 1994. "VR Projects at Germany's Fraunhofer Institutes." *Virtual Reality World* 2(6):30–32.

Shaw, Jeffrey. 1991. "Das Virtuelle Museum." In Manfred Waffender (Ed.), *Cyberspace: Ausflüge in Virtuelle Wirklichkeiten.* Reinbek bei Hamburg: Rowohlt, p. 155.

Sheridan, Thomas. 1992. "Defining Our Terms." *Presence: Teleoperators and Virtual Environments* 1(2):272–274.

Shotton, Margaret. 1989. *Computer Addiction? A Study of Computer Dependency.* London: Taylor and Francis.

Silverstone, Roger. 1994. *Television and Everyday Life.* London: Routledge.

Silverstone, Roger, and Eric Hirsch (Eds.). 1992. *Consuming Technologies: Media and Information in Domestic Spaces.* London: Routledge.

Silverstone, Roger, and Leslie Haddon. 1993. "Future Compatible? Information and Communication Technologies in the Home: A Methodology and a Case Study." A report prepared for the Commission of the European Communities Socioeconomic and Technical Impact Assessments and Forecasts, RACE Project 2086. Science Policy Research Unit, University of Sussex.

Slater, Mel, and Martin Usoh. 1993. "The Influence of a Virtual Body on Presence in Immersive Virtual Environments." In Tony Feldman (Ed.), *VR93—Proceedings of the Third Annual Conference on Virtual Reality.* London: Meckler, pp. 34–42.

Slater, Mel, Martin Usoh, and Anthony Steed. 1994. "Depth of Presence in Virtual Environments." *Presence: Teleoperators and Virtual Environments* 3(2):130–144.

Smith, Merritt Roe, and Leo Marx (Eds.). 1994. *Does Technology Drive History? The Dilemma of Technological Determinism.* Cambridge, Mass.: MIT Press.

Smith, Roger D. 1994. "Current Military Simulations and the Integration of Virtual Reality Technologies." *Virtual Reality World* 2(2):45–50.

Sorlin, Pierre. 1994. *Mass Media.* London: Routledge.

Sprout, Randy. 1993. "Virtual Reality Entertainment Developers: An Industry Overview." *Pix-elation* 2(2):8–22.

Stallings, William, and Richard van Slyke. 1994 (second edition). *Business Data Communication.* Englewood Cliffs: Macmillan.

Stefanac, Suzanne. 1993. "Interactive Hollywood." *New Media* 3(8):40–48.

Stenger, Nicole. 1992. "Real-Time Movies: A New Industry." *Interface to Real and Virtual Worlds.* Paris: EC2, pp. 37–38.

Sterling, Bruce. 1993. "War Is Virtual Hell." *Wired* 1(1):46–51 and 94–99.

Steuer, Jonathan. 1995. "Defining Virtual Reality: Dimensions Determining Telepresence." In Frank Biocca and Mark Levy (Eds.), *Communication in the Age of Virtual Reality.* Hillsdale, N.J.: Lawrence Erlbaum Associates, pp. 33–56.

Stone, Alluquere Rosanne. 1991. "Will the Real Body Please Stand Up?: Boundary Stories about Virtual Cultures." In Michael Benedikt (Ed.), *Cyberspace: First Steps.* Cambridge, Mass.: MIT Press, pp. 81–118.

Stone, Robert. 1994. "A Year in the Life of British Virtual Reality." *Virtual Reality World* 2(1), pp. 48–62.

Stone, Valerie. 1993. "Social Interaction and Social Development in Virtual Environments." *Presence: Teleoperators and Virtual Environments* 2(2):153–161.

Stytz, Martin R. 1994. "An Overview of Current Virtual Reality Research and Development Projects by the United States Department of Defense." In Sandra Helsel (Ed.), *Proceedings of the Fourth Annual Conference on Virtual Reality* London: Meckler, pp. 152–159.

Stytz, Martin, et al. 1995. "Portraying and Understanding Large-Scale Distributed Virtual Environments: Experience and Tentative Conclusions." *Presence: Teleoperators and Virtual Environments* 4(2):146–168.

Sutherland, Ivan. 1965. "The Ultimate Display." *Proceedings of the International Federation of Information Processing Congress*, pp. 506–508.

Sutherland, Ivan. 1968. "A Head-Mounted Three Dimensional Display." *Proceedings of the Fall Joint Computer Conference*, pp. 757–764.

Tachi, Susumu, and Kenichi Yasuda. 1994. "Evaluation Experiments of a Teleexistence Manipulation System." *Presence: Teleoperators and Virtual Environments* 3(1):35–44.

Taylor II, Russell, et al. 1993. "The Nanomanipulator: A Virtual Reality Interface for a Scanning Tunneling Microscope." *Computer Graphics Proceedings, Annual Conference Series*, pp. 127–134.

Tesler, Lawrence. 1991. "Networked Computing in the 1990s." *Scientific American* 265(3):54–61.

Thompson, Jeremy. 1993. *Virtual Reality: An International Directory of Research Projects*. Aldershot: JBT Publishing.

Tran, Mark. 1993. "Toying With the Next Generation of Media." *The Guardian*, July 29, p. 17.

Trigg, Roger. 1993. *Rationality and Science: Can Science Explain Everything?*. Oxford: Blackwell.

U.S. Congress, Office of Technology Assessment. 1994. *Virtual Reality and Technologies for Combat Simulation—Background Paper, OTA-BP-ISS-136*. Washington, D.C.: U.S. Government Printing Office.

Vince, John. 1992. "Virtual Reality Techniques in Flight Simulation." In Huw Jones and Mike Gigante (Eds.), *Virtual Reality Systems—Proceedings of the British Computer Society Displays Group Conference*, London (no pp.).

Vincent, John, and Susan Wyshinski. 1994. "Mirror World." In Sandra Helsel (Ed.), *Proceedings of the Fourth Annual Conference on Virtual Reality*. London: Meckler, pp. 15–29.

VR News. Cydata Ltd, PO Box 2515, London N4 4JW.

Walker, Margaret. 1987. "The Makaton Vocabulary: Uses and Effectiveness." Paper to AFAISIC Symposium.

Watson, Benjamin. 1994. "A Survey of Virtual Reality in Japan." *Presence: Teleoperators and Virtual Environments* 3(1):1–18.

Watts, Susan, and Michael Leapman. 1993. "BBC's News Bulletins Move into Virtual Reality." *The Independent*, April 7, p. 6.

Weber, Max. 1948. *From Max Weber: Essays in Sociology*. London: Routledge and Kegan Paul.

Weber, Max. 1949. *The Methodology of the Social Sciences*. Glencoe, Ill.: Free Press.

Weber, Max. 1980 (fourth edition). *Gesammelte Politische Schriften*. Tübingen: J.C.B. Mohr.

Wenzel, Elizabeth. 1992. "Localization in Virtual Acoustic Displays." *Presence: Teleoperators and Virtual Environments* 1(1):80–107.

Whittingdon, Amanda. 1992. "Fun with Eric the Spider." *New Statesman and Society*, May 29, p. 33.

Winn, William, and William Bricken. 1992. "Designing Virtual Worlds for Use in Mathematics Education: The Example of Experiential Algebra." *Educational Technology*, December, pp. 12–19.

Winner, Langdon. 1986. "Mythinformation." In his *The Whale and the Reactor—A Search for Limits in an Age of High Technology*. Chicago: The University of Chicago Press, pp. 98–117.

Wiseman, Bill. 1992. "Furness Speaks Before Senate Hearing." *HITLab Review* 1:8–9.

Wood, Claire, and Ian Gwalter. 1995. "Communicating Emotions Using Virtual Reality." Paper presented at the Royal Society Conference on Virtual Reality in Society, Engineering and Science, London.

Woolley, Benjamin. 1992. *Virtual Worlds: A Journey in Hype and Hyperreality*. Oxford: Blackwell.

Woolgar, Steve. 1988. *Science: The Very Idea*. Chichester: Ellis Horwood.

Woolgar, Steve. 1991. "The Turn to Technology in the Social Studies of Science." *Science, Technology, and Human Values* 16(1):20–50.

Zeltzer, David. 1992. "Autonomy, Interaction, and Presence." *Presence: Teleoperators and Virtual Environments* 1(1):127–132.

Zyda, Michael, et al. 1993. "NPSNET and the Naval Postgraduate School Graphics and Video Laboratory." *Presence: Teleoperators and Virtual Environments* 2(3):244–258.

About the Book and Author

Virtual reality has rapidly become one of the most exciting new computer technologies—exercising a strong hold on the popular imagination, attracting hundreds of researchers, and spawning a booming industry. This study explores the social implications of VR technology. It traces the history of VR and then relates it to general issues in the study of the effects of new information and communication technologies. The book examines VR's relationship to advanced research and development, to education and the entertainment industries, and finally to cyberpunk and youth culture. It also challenges conventional ideas in the sociology of science and technology and develops a realist and Weberian approach to the social dynamic of new technologies. *Possible Worlds* is the first book to examine the social aspects of virtual reality and provides a comprehensive understanding of this complex technology.

Ralph Schroeder is lecturer in sociology at Royal Holloway, University of London.

Index